YORK NOTES

The Miller's Prologue and Tale

Geoffrey Chaucer

Note by Pamela M. King

 Longman   York Press

Pamela M. King is hereby identified as author of this work in accordance with
Section 77 of the Copyright, Designs and Patents Act 1988

YORK PRESS
322 Old Brompton Road, London SW5 9JH

PEARSON EDUCATION LIMITED
Edinburgh Gate, Harlow,
Essex CM20 2JE, United Kingdom
Associated companies, branches and representatives throughout the world

First published 2000

ISBN 0-582-42461-5

Designed by Vicki Pacey
Phototypeset by Gem Graphics, Trenance, Mawgan Porth, Cornwall
Colour reproduction and film output by Spectrum Colour
Produced by Addison Wesley Longman China Limited, Hong Kong

CONTENTS

PART ONE

INTRODUCTION

HOW TO STUDY A NARRATIVE POEM

Studying a narrative poem on your own requires self-discipline and a carefully thought-out work plan in order to be effective.

- You will need to read the poem more than once. Start by reading it quickly for pleasure, then read it slowly and thoroughly.

- Look up all the words which you do not know. Some may have more than one meaning so note them.

- On your second reading make detailed notes on the plot, characters and themes. Further readings will generate new ideas.

- Think about how the poem is narrated. From whose point of view are the events described? Does your response to the narrator change at all in the course of the poem?

- The main character is the narrator, but what about the others? Do they develop? Do you only ever see them from the narrator's point of view?

- Identify what styles of language are used in the poem.

- Assess what the main arguments are in the poem. Who are the narrator's main opponents? Are their views ever fairly presented?

- Are words, images or incidents repeated so as to give the work a pattern? Do such patterns help you to understand the poem's themes?

- What is the effect of the poem's ending? Is the action completed and closed, or left incomplete and open?

- Does the poem present a world or point of view of which you are meant to approve?

- Cite exact sources for all quotations. Wherever possible find your own examples to back up your opinions.

- Always express your ideas in your own words.

This York Note offers an introduction to *The Miller's Prologue and Tale* and cannot substitute for close reading of the text and the study of secondary sources.

Chaucer's Miller unceremoniously blunders into the genteel story-telling competition in *The Canterbury Tales*. The tone has just been set by the Knight, and everyone else is supposed to follow according to rank. The Miller insists he should go next as he has a story which will follow *The Knight's Tale* aptly. *The Knight's Tale* is an aristocratic tale of chivalry, set in ancient Thebes, telling the story of how two brothers, Palamon and Arcite compete for the hand of fair Emily. It includes fine speeches, pagan gods and goddesses, and culminates in a splendid tournament, described in great detail. How can the Miller, an ugly oafish sort of man, so drunk that even he notices that he is slurring his words, possibly follow that? It seems safe to assume that the Miller has neither the skill in story-telling, nor the experience of life, to be able to match the Knight, even if he can remain upright.

Nevertheless, the genial host of the pilgrimage, Harry Bailey, a publican by trade – so well accustomed to handling belligerent drunks – eventually gives way. *The Miller's Tale* which follows is a remarkable extended dirty joke. There is a beautiful lady, the saucy Alison, wife of old John the Oxford carpenter. There are two competing lovers, Nicholas the student lodger, clever but idle, and the rather precious Absolon, parish clerk and local barber, who has an interesting hairstyle and a horror of farting. The plot is complex, weaving together two practical jokes, one involving the rebuilding of Noah's ark, the other concerned with getting Absolon to kiss Alison's bare backside. The reader is thrown into bewilderment wondering how it will all end, little anticipating the single-word punchline. Small-town life in medieval Oxford is set out in the same loving detail with which the characters are described. Much of the action is frankly rude, and in the end everyone seems to get their just deserts, but just how seriously should the reader take it all?

How can this Miller, who uses his head to break down doors, have the mental equipment to tell such a good story, even sober? Where is Chaucer in all this? He has told his readers that he was on the pilgrimage himself and will tell each pilgrim's story exactly as he heard it, but the pilgrimage is itself a fiction. What, then, is Chaucer up to, when he tells his readers before the Miller begins that, if they are not keen on the type of tale the Miller is likely to tell, they should skip a page and choose something else? What, in the end, *is* the relationship between *The Miller's Tale* and *The Knight's Tale*? And what makes the Reeve so angry, that he tells an even ruder tale about a miller next in the sequence?

PART TWO

COMMENTARIES

The Miller's Prologue and Tale *is the second of Chaucer's* Canterbury Tales, *the long sequence of framed stories which he was working on when he died. No version survives in Chaucer's own handwriting. Printing had not been invented when Chaucer wrote, so the earliest versions of* The Canterbury Tales *are all in manuscripts written by scribes for purchasers with different requirements. No two manuscripts are identical. It is not altogether clear which order Chaucer intended for the Tales, but in all complete or near-complete early manuscripts the book begins with* the General Prologue, *followed by* The Knight's Tale, The Miller's Tale *and* The Reeve's Tale.

The standard edition of the complete works of Chaucer is Larry D. Benson, ed., The Riverside Chaucer, Houghton Mifflin, 1987. *These notes are based on the single edition of* The Miller's Prologue and Tale, *ed. James Winny, Cambridge University Press, 1971.*

SYNOPSIS

The Miller introduced in the *General Prologue* is a thickset thug, accomplished at wrestling and playing the bagpipes, known as a loud-mouth, and travelling armed. He bursts into the story-telling contest once the pilgrimage gets underway, claiming that he can tell a story to match the Knight's with which the competition has begun. He is drunk, and cannot be deflected from his purpose, so for the sake of peace he is allowed to go ahead. Chaucer intervenes in his own voice at the end of *The Miller's Prologue* to warn his readers that the Miller was drunk, that his Tale is not in very refined taste. It is, in fact, permissible to skip this Tale altogether.

The Tale is set in Oxford, at the boarding house of a rich carpenter, John. He has, as his lodger, a poor student, Nicholas, who has a passion for astronomy. John, though old, has recently married Alison, who is eighteen. She is rather wild, tall, slender and pretty, so John lives in fear that she will cuckold him, for he loves her dearly.

Nicholas finds Alison irresistible, and one day while John is away from home, talks her into agreeing to sleep with him whenever they can contrive the opportunity. Alison then collects another admirer, Absolon, the rather fastidious parish clerk. Absolon too sets about wooing Alison, by playing his guitar under her bedroom window at night, sending her presents, and swearing undying service. Alison favours Nicholas.

John goes away to work at Oseney, so Nicholas and Alison put their plan into action. John gets back to find Nicholas apparently in a trance in his room. When the door is broken down and John has said various charms over him, Nicholas revives and confides that he has learned that a second Flood is coming in a couple of days' time. If John wishes to save his wife and Nicholas, he must hang from the rafters three tubs, in which they will sleep, floating out on the waters when everyone else has drowned. John makes preparations accordingly.

Meanwhile Absolon's wooing continues. On the very night Nicholas and Alison are in bed together, having climbed out of their tubs, leaving John asleep in the roof, Absolon turns up at the bedroom window asking for a kiss. Alison eventually agrees if he will go away, but sticks her bare backside out of the window in the dark. Absolon kisses it, realises his mistake, swears revenge and borrows a red hot iron from a neighbouring blacksmith. He then returns and asks for another kiss. This time it is Nicholas who sticks his backside out of the window. He gets badly burned and immediately shouts for water. Up in the roof John hears, and believes the Flood has come, so he cuts the ropes holding up his tub. Instead of floating safely away, he plummets to the ground and breaks his arm. Attracted by the commotion, all the neighbours come round and have a good laugh.

THE MILLER IN *THE GENERAL PROLOGUE*

His dastardly character makes him an odd sort of pilgrim

The Miller was a large, strong, thickset and muscular man, with a red beard, a wide nose on which there is a wart that also sprouts red hairs, and a mouth like a furnace. He frequently won prizes for wrestling, we are told, and could knock doors off their hinges or open them by charging them with his head. He was a blabbermouth and teller of dirty stories. He stole corn from his customers as well as trebling his commission; he had a talent for making money. On the pilgrimage he was armed with a sword and shield, wore a white coat and blue hood, and piped his companions out of London on his bagpipes.

The description of the Miller is constructed from alliterating short Anglo-Saxon words, conveying a sense of his crudeness and physicality which is borne out by the details of his physical appearance. Most of the details in the description can be related to moral and psychological attributes through the voguish medieval science of physiognomy (see Characterisation). Everyone had to take their grain for grinding to the miller in a village community. A miller, like a reeve – a bailiff or overseer of the manor – had both the power and the opportunity for operating sharp business practices. This Miller also has physical power, exercised in wrestling, a sport much disapproved of by the church, and is travelling armed. Combine that finally with the power of the gossip and you have a portrait of a rather unholy pilgrim whose company many might wish to avoid. Yet there is something of the carnival character (see Critical History, on Carnival) about him as he pipes the pilgrims out of Southwark on his bagpipes. The bagpipes were considered a rather ungenteel instrument in the Middle Ages, appearing in pictures either of village revelries or of devils playing them in hell.

carl churl
for the nones for the time (relatively meaningless filler)
he wolde have alwey the ram he always took the prize (traditionally a live ram)

short-sholdred thick-set
knarre knot (as in wood)
harre hinges
janglere teller of dirty stories
goliardeys buffoon
tollen thries charge treble commission
a thombe of golde a way with money
pardee by God

THE MILLER'S PROLOGUE

LINES 1–78   In which it is agreed who will tell a Tale after the Knight

Everyone was delighted with the Knight's Tale. Harry Bailey invited the Monk to continue with his story. The Miller, so drunk that he could hardly sit on his horse, interrupted in a loud voice. The Host tried to pacify him but eventually gave way and let him go next to avoid trouble. Before beginning his Tale, however, the Miller apologised to the assembled company. He knew he was drunk, so the company should blame not him but Southwark ale if he said anything amiss. He promised to tell the story of how a student got a carpenter's wife into bed. The Reeve, a carpenter by trade, butted in, enraged at the prospect of such a story. The Miller attempted to pacify him by admitting that he was married himself, and that he thought there were more good wives than bad. At any rate, he said, men should not enquire too closely into their wives' business, any more than they should God's. Chaucer intervenes in his own voice, warning his readers that the Miller was an uncouth sort of man, and his Tale may offend. You can skip it, he says, and choose another Tale, as there is something in *The Canterbury Tales* to suit all tastes, so don't blame him if you make the wrong choice.

The *Prologue* of *The Miller's Tale* takes the form of a conversation between Harry Bailey and the Miller. Harry Bailey is the landlord of the Tabard Inn from which the pilgrims set out, and the man credited with setting up the story-telling contest in the first place, the Host. The Tale of the Knight, who went first, was an aristocratic **Romance** telling of the competing love of two young men for a beautiful girl, resolved in a grand tournament. The Host asks for something to 'quite with' it, which can have two senses, either 'to balance' or 'to pay back'. It seems the Host intends the first sense, but the Miller, by line 19, is intent on the second. The Monk is invited to go next because the Host wants a 'better man' than the Miller, an uncontroversial reference at the period to the Miller's rank in society, but also a potential snub referring to his manners and morals. The Miller is portrayed as very uncouth as well as drunk, shouting in the voice traditionally associated with the character of Pilate in mystery plays. Mystery plays, the urban religious dramas played and sponsored by townspeople in celebration of the annual feast of Corpus Christi, will recur in *The Miller's Tale* (line 276). His intrusion not only disturbs the order of the story-telling, but provokes strife among the pilgrims, as the Reeve takes the proposed subject of the Tale personally. The Miller's views on marriage which follow give some indication as to how his Tale will treat relationships between the sexes. They represent a shift in tone from the preceding Tale in which women are pure, beautiful, virginal and unattainable and men are strong, brave and courteous (see Themes, on Love), to one where women are devious and unfaithful and men best not to enquire too closely into their wives' affairs. His warning that men should not probe into their wives' private affairs any more than into God's is **proleptic** of the major theme of the Tale that follows (see Narrative Techniques, on Diction). Chaucer's intervention foregrounds the narrative artifice of *The Canterbury Tales* (see Characterisation, on Chaucer the Ventriloquist). He flatters the readers by assuming that they, like those who have enjoyed *The Knight's Tale*, are people of refined taste. The final instruction that no-one should take fun too seriously, coupled with the disruption of order provoked by the Miller, also suggest that the tale-telling competition is moving into the world of carnival and in danger of subversion (see Critical History, on Carnival).

2 **route** company
5 **namely** particularly
  gentils high-ranking people

6 **So moot I gon** upon my life
7 **unbokeled is the male** the bag is open
13 **unnethe** scarcely
14 **nolde avalen** would not take off
15 **abide** wait for
21 **leeve** dear
29 **protestacioun** justification
30 **soun** voice
32 **Wite** understand
35 **set the wrightes cappe** make a fool of the carpenter
36 **Stint thy clappe** stop your noise
39 **apeyren** damage
49 **artow** are you
53 **demen** judge
56 **privetee** private affairs
57 **foison** abundance
71 **storial** history-like

THE MILLER'S TALE

LINES 78–112   Carpenter takes attractive student lodger with an
                interest in astrology

Once in Oxford there lived a carpenter, a rich man, who ran a boarding
house. He took as a lodger a poor student called Nicholas. Nicholas was
no trouble, solitary, neat and tidy in his personal habits. He was
particularly interested in astronomy and had lots of books on the
subject up in his room. Every evening Nicholas played the psaltery,
a soft-sounding stringed instrument, and sang very sweetly.

> Chaucer knew Oxford well and so did his audience, though the
> picture of Oxford and its environs presented in the Tale strongly
> suggests that, for London-based Chaucer and his audience, Oxford
> provided a location for poking fun at provincial life. Oxford
> University, however, was also a place where astronomy was a very
> popular area of investigation at the period, and one in which
> Chaucer had an amateur interest (see Background, on Chaucer's
> Oxford). The picture of Nicholas distracted from his studies by

astronomy would have been the matter of a topical joke. He is officially studying the arts which made up the basic university syllabus. There were seven: the 'trivium' – logic, rhetoric and dialectic – and the 'quadrivium' – astronomy, arithmetic, geometry and music. Chaucer accentuates the attraction of obscure sciences by using polysyllabic words to end the lines which introduce this arcane subject. Nicholas's name may connect him to Saint Nicholas, the patron saint of sweet smells and of young girls, but may also connect him with a famous Oxford astrologer (see Background, on Chaucer's Oxford). From the outset he is also described as 'hende', almost as if it were part of his name. The adjective is symptomatic of one of Chaucer's major literary techniques in the Tale as it can mean both 'courteous' and 'handy' (see Narrative Techniques, on Diction). Nicholas is, for Alison, both. His way of life is private and secretive, both of which will also become important ideas as the Tale progresses. Initially, however, the reader simply notes that, unlike most students, he has a room to himself which he keeps as sweet and neat as he does his own person. The room contains his books, his bed and his musical instrument, which represent his main preoccupations. His favourite song is one associated with the Annunciation, when the angel Gabriel came to the Virgin Mary while her husband was away and invited her to conceive the child of God (see Themes). The passage concludes with the satirical suggestion that Nicholas wastes his time to a degree which depends upon his current income and the subsidies of his friends. Every detail in this passage sets up in one way or another the lines of plot and the verbal jokes upon which the rest of the Tale will depend as it unfolds.

80 **gnof** churl
gestes heeld to bord took in paying guests
85 **koude a certain of conclusiouns** could carry out experiments
86 **demen by interrogaciouns** judge by enquiries
91 **cleped** called
92 **deerne** secret
93 **sleigh** cunning
privee discreet

97 **fetisly ydight** elegantly decorated
99 **cetewale** setwall (a spice like ginger)
100 **Almageste** astrology textbook
101 **astrelabie** astrolabe (astronomical instrument on which Chaucer wrote a
treatise)
longinge for belonging to
102 **augrim stones** arithmetical counters
104 **presse** cupboard
a falding reed a red woollen blanket
105 **sautrie** psaltery (stringed instrument)
108 ***Angelus ad virginem*** *The Angel to the Virgin*
109 **the Kinges Noote** unidentified song about the king

LINES 113–24   The carpenter had made a bad marriage to a flighty
young girl

John, an old carpenter had married an eighteen-year-old girl, completely
ignoring the stock advice that man should marry his equal. He loved her
and so now, fearing she would be unfaithful to him, jealously kept her a
virtual prisoner.

> John from the outset is portrayed not only as old but as unlearned
> and, by implication, stupid. He may not have read Dionysius Cato's
> fourth-century *Disticha de Moribus ad Filium* (Treatise about
> Customs for Sons), but common sense should have told him this
> marriage was fated. The bringing together of the doltish carpenter
> with a great classical philosopher, or even the suggestion that
> members of the working classes ought to be reading Cato, is the
> source of the passage's **irony**. Is Chaucer laughing at the carpenter
> for not being well read, or at himself for bookish irrelevance in areas
> where common sense should prevail? Before the reader meets
> Alison she is described **proleptically** as 'wilde' as well as young. In
> many of the Tale's **fabliaux** sources (see Literary Background) the
> wife is literally a prisoner; here the **imagery** suggests that the
> marriage is a trap for both partners. John keeps her in a
> **metaphorical** cage, but he has himself fallen into a 'snare' by
> marrying her in the first place. Later in the Tale he will be literally
> caught in a trap in his own rafters.

116 **narwe** closely
119 **Catoun** Cato
122 **at debaat** at odds

LINES 125–62 The wife is described

Alison was pretty, tall and slender. She dressed elaborately in black and white silk. She shone like a newly forged coin and carried a decorated purse at her waist. She was lively, had a roving eye and a loud, shrill singing voice. She is compared to young animals, fruits and flowers and, in conclusion, is considered a suitable mistress for a lord, or wife for a farmer.

See Extended Commentaries, Text 1.

127 **ceint** girdle
128 **barmclooth** apron
129 **lendes ... goore** her skirt is very full around her hips, made up of lots of gores of fabric
133 **voluper** cap
135 **filet** headband
136 **likerous** lecherous
140 **pere-jonette** early-ripening variety of pear
143 **perled with latoun** decorated with brass
145 **thenche** think of
146 **popelote** pet
148 **noble** small gold coin
149 **yerne** lively
153 **bragot or the meeth** ale mixed with honey, or mead
155 **Winsinge** skittish
158 **the boos of a bokeler** the central boss of a shield
160 **piggesnie** a joke. Literally 'pig's eye', Chaucer invents a wild flower on the lines of 'ox-eye' or 'day's-eye' (daisy)

LINES 163–98 Nicholas makes his first move to seduce Alison while John is away from home

One day when John was out of town, Nicholas grabbed Alison and told her he would die if he could not have her. She told him to get his hands off her, but he talked her round and she promised to do what he wanted when the opportunity arose. She was afraid of what the jealous John would do if he caught them, and made Nicholas swear to be discreet, but he was confident that a scholar could outwit a carpenter. In the meantime he played her a tune on his psaltery to celebrate their arrangement.

It is not clear why Alison plays so hard to get in her first encounter with Nicholas unless to build comic suspense. The passage incongruously juxtaposes speech and action. What Nicholas says draws on the language of **courtly love**, where the lover claims to be dying of love, swears to be discreet and to preserve the lady's honour. He does, however, call her his 'lemman', a term which had become overused in Middle English literature in sexual contexts and thus probably made it clear from the outset that Nicholas's plea was explicitly for sexual favours. 'Spille', meaning 'die' in a courtly context may here also be a *double entendre* implying that he will have an orgasm. At any rate, she denies him a kiss and cries out more in the language of a victim of rape or murder than a girl being seduced. She is then won round with indecorous haste. She swears by Saint Thomas à Becket, the patron saint of Oseney where John is busy working as carpenter on the abbey, but also the martyred monk to whose shrine the *Canterbury Tales'* pilgrims are travelling. While he is pleading, and she spurning him, he is 'queynte' – subtle – enough to grab her by the 'queynte' – private parts – an example of *rime riche* (see Narrative Techniques, on Diction), hold her by her hipbones, pat her bottom, and eventually to kiss her. By the time he plays his psaltery to her at the end of the encounter his melody-making has distinct sexual connotations, anticipating the 'melody' they will later make in John's bed (line 544). The focus on Alison's lower body anticipates the moment when she will stick her backside out of the window into Absolon's waiting face when he too begs a kiss (lines 624–9).

167-8 **queynte ... queynte** subtle ... private parts
170 **lemman** sweetheart (low status)
    spille die
174 **trave** frame for restraining horses
178 **'out, harrow'** cry of distress associated with extreme tragedy

179 **for youre curteisie** if you please

183 **Seint Thomas of Kent** St Thomas à Becket, martyred archbishop of Canterbury and popular local English saint

191 **litherly biset his while** wasted his time

196 **thakked** patted

lendes thighs, buttocks

LINES 199–243 Parish clerk Absolon falls for Alison in church

Then one holy day Alison went to church, where she caught the eye of a parish clerk called Absolon. He had a pink face, eyes grey as a goose, and carefully parted curly blond hair like a fan. He was neatly dressed and very clean. He wore red stockings and a pale blue tunic, held together with lots of elaborate lacing. Over that he had a pure white surplice. He had cut-outs in his shoes like church windows. He also had a range of accomplishments as a barber-surgeon and a draughtsman of minor legal documents. He knew twenty dances, played guitar and fiddle, and sang falsetto around the local bars. He was fastidious about his speech and squeamish about farting. Absolon was going about wafting the local ladies with incense and making eyes at them. He found Alison so sexy that he wished he was a cat and she a mouse so he could catch her. He was so lovesick that he refused to take the collection.

Alison's visit to church is undertaken as part of the normal civic Christian's duty to attend on particular holy days. As she leaves, she crosses herself with holy water, as was usual. Here it is suggested, however, that this makes her forehead shine in such a way as to make her irresistible to Absolon, which is mildly blasphemous, or at least indicates the turn the Tale is going to take. The description of Absolon, like that of Alison, represents a departure from the normal narrative structure of the **fabliau** (see Literary Background). Again it depends on the accumulation of detail and **imagery** to create its effect. He is associated with Absalom in the Old Testament (2 Samuel) who was hanged by his luxuriant hair in an oak tree.

Absolon's appearance is poised between the outlandish and the effeminate. As with the description of Alison, the images of comparison draw on the homely domestic world which the characters inhabit. Absolon's accomplishments are varied, but are all associated with small-town activity and do not require the level of scholarship in which Nicholas is, at least theoretically, involved. In particular, Absolon's job as a barber-surgeon both reminds us of his own excess of hair and will later explain how it is that he can be certain that women do not have beards (line 629). His activity of censing draws attention to the Tale's focus on smell imagery. The activity may be a **metaphor** for the kind of sanitised sexual activity about which Absolon fantasises, and therefore joins the Tale's many sexual innuendos. His squeamishness about farting is also **proleptic** of his two stolen 'kisses' at the window when he goes wooing in the dark (lines 626 and 698–9).

205 **ycleped** called

207 **strouted** stuck out

208 **shode** parting

209 **rode** complexion

210 **Poules window corven on his shoos** he had cut-outs in his shoes in the shape of church (St Paul's) windows

211 **fetisly** elegantly

213 **kirtel** tunic

waget pale blue fabric

214 **Ful faire ... pointes set** a profusion of laces attached his stockings to his tunic

216 **ris** bough

218 **laten blood** open veins for medicinal purposes

219 **acquitaunce** receipt or deed

223 **rubible** early fiddle (rebeck)

224 **quinible** high voice

225 **giterne** early guitar

228 **gailard tappestere** jolly landlord

230 **daungerous** haughty

232 **sencer** vessel for swinging incense in church

LINES 244–61   Absolon goes wooing

That moonlit night, Absolon took his guitar and arrived at the carpenter's house in the early hours of the morning. He stood by a hinged window in the house wall and sang a sweet love song. John woke and asked Alison if she had heard; she replied that she had. Neither of them did anything about it.

> This brief passage moves the plot along. Absolon aspires to be a courtly lover (see Themes, on Love), judging by the words of his song. Chaucer prepares us for this by using the word 'paramours', a pretentious, and somewhat overused, French term popular in Romance narratives. But the true courtly lover woos secretly and discreetly. Here it is the husband, not his lady, whom he awakes with his love song. Moreover John immediately recognises Absolon's voice, possibly because of its high pitch, and wakes Alison to hear. The effect is to indicate Absolon's complete failure, as not only does his song reach the wrong pair of ears, but the husband and wife's companionable recognition of who is singing at their window suggests that neither of them takes Absolon's suit particularly seriously or perceives it as a threat. The passage does, however, introduce the audience to the 'shot-windowe', the latest in urban housing improvements, a large glazed window set low in the wall and hinged to open like a door. This will be vital to the plot as it later unfolds.

246 **paramours he thoghte for to wake**   he decided to stay up all night for love's sake

250 **dressed him up**   set himself up

254 **rewe**   have pity

255 **acordaunt**   in harmony with

259 **boures wal**   bedroom wall

LINES 262–90   **Absolon keeps trying to win Alison to no avail**

Absolon continued to devote himself to Alison. Unable to sleep, he did all he could to win her, attending to his good grooming, singing to her, sending her presents of food and money. He played Herod in the mystery plays. All was to no avail, for she loved Nicholas and so made a fool of Absolon. The fact that Nicholas lived in the same house as she did meant that Absolon really did not have a chance.

All the pains that Absolon takes to win Alison are described in detail, while it is also made clear that his efforts are wasted since Nicholas has won her simply by being in constant close proximity, handy (see Narrative Techniques, on Diction). As the narrator puts it proverbially, 'the sly person nearby makes the far-away lover seem repulsive'. Absolon may as well 'blow the buck's horn', that is, he is wasting his time. This passage is full of proverbial expressions as the voice of the narrator seems to **parody** that of a middle-aged matchmaker, possibly in echo of Criseyde's fussy uncle Pandarus in Chaucer's long **Romance**, *Troilus and Criseyde*. The gifts Absolon lavishes on Alison speak eloquently of their social status (see Themes, on Social Climbing): he gives her food, ale and money rather than the exotica a knight might offer his beloved. The narrator comments again, however, that some women are won by wealth, some by rough treatment and some by fine manners. The suggestion seems to be that a woman of Alison's social status might well be attracted by money. It is also a veiled allusion to women's proverbial fickleness which echoes *The Wife of Bath's Tale*, where the knight on a quest to find out what women really want is given a variety of similar answers. At any rate, Absolon's wooing is both inept and in keeping with the petit-bourgeois world the characters inhabit. It is undertaken through intermediaries and brokers as if he were trying to conclude a deal on a piece of property. One of the things he does to impress her is to play the part of Herod in the mystery plays. Mystery plays were performed and sponsored by the trade and craftsmen in medieval cities to celebrate religious festivals, particularly Corpus Christi day. Herod and Pilate – remember the Miller himself speaks with Pilate's voice – were the great villains, designed to be played in **bombastic** manner. Absolon, judging by his appearance and what we already know of his voice, is better equipped to play female roles, something which some men must have specialised in, given that there is no evidence that women performed. Contemporary records also reveal that parish clerks played an active role all over the country in these amateur theatricals.

267 **meenes** go-betweens
    brocage agents
269 **brokkinge** quavering
270 **piment** spiced wine
    meeth mead
272 **he profred meede** offered her money
274 **strokes** violence
276 **upon a scaffold hye** on an outdoor stage
282 **jape** joke

LINES 291–339   **John goes out of town; Nicholas and Alison put their plan into action**

One Saturday, John again went to Oseney and Nicholas and Alison put a plan into action that would allow them to spend a night together. Nicholas took two days' food and drink to his room and she agreed to pretend that she had not seen him and was afraid he was ill. John, returning on Sunday evening, began to worry about his lodger's well-being, mindful of how unexpectedly death can strike, so he sent his servant to bang on Nicholas's door. The servant was unable to rouse Nicholas but eventually managed to look into the room through a hole in the skirting through which the cat came and went. He saw Nicholas apparently in a trance, so went to tell John.

> Nicholas and Alison's plot which will allow them to sleep together is described in great detail. Particularly apt is the information that there is a hole low in the wall of Nicholas's room, regularly used by the cat. We recall that Absolon wished he were a cat and Alison a mouse so he could catch her. The inclusion of the cat-flap detail at this point in the plot suggests by metonymy how cat-like Nicholas is: as ever, what Absolon wants to be, Nicholas already is. The passage also begins to flesh out John's character. His concern for Nicholas seems genuine, but his doom-mongering about sudden death, and our knowledge that he is so easily tricked, preserve a certain distance. With John, as with all the characters in the Tale, our sympathies are engaged just enough to keep us interested in what happens to him, but not quite enough to make us care. John's account of the man who was at work on Monday and buried on

Sunday is the kind of reminder of death which had become rather a cliché of popular religion in the plague-ridden towns of the fourteenth century. It is also one of the main points of departure for the plot of *The Pardoner's Tale.*

295 **shapen him a wile** formed a cunning plan

302 **dooth ful softe ... carie** had very discreetly taken

306 **niste** did not know

310 **He nolde answere for thing that mighte falle** he would not answer whatever happened

313 **dide what him leste** pleased himself

315 **merveile** wonder

317 **adrad** fearful

318 **It stondeth nat aright** all is not well

320 **tikel** unpredictable

sikerly truly

324 **Clepe** call out

336 **caping upright** gaping into the air

337 **kiked** gazed

339 **array** state

LINES 340–63   John speculates on Nicholas's problem and arranges his rescue

John speculates piously on what might have happened to Nicholas, blaming his ambition to know God's secrets. He tells of a man who walked around gazing at the stars and fell into a clay-pit by not looking where he was going. The servant goes and breaks Nicholas's door down.

There are two jokes being sustained in this passage. The first is internal to the plot (see Narrative Techniques, on Diction) and involves John's proleptic warning about how prying into the future and seeking to understand God's secrets will lead to a fall. The Miller has already warned in his *Prologue* that a man should not enquire into either God's 'privetee' or his wife's, drawing attention to the double meaning of the word which also means 'private parts'. Curiosity about both God's and woman's 'privetee' will cause trouble later in the Tale (see Narrative Techniques, on Diction). John tells the cautionary tale, drawn from ancient Greek but often retold, of the star-gazer who fell into the well. Here the well becomes a clay-pit, of which there were many in the vicinity of Oxford. The story's original moral is directed against those foolish enough to believe that the future could be read from the stars. This does not prevent John from later believing Nicholas's highly improbable star-gazer's prediction that he has been singled out as the second Noah. He will, as a result, sustain a painful fall himself. The second joke connects the values of the Tale, and the intellectual capacities of the characters, with the Miller himself. John's diatribe against too much studying led him to bless the ignorant man. The solution to the immediate problem is also to apply brute strength, and the servant, called Robin just like the Miller, demonstrates that he too is adept at knocking down doors. Thus not only does the Tale set the learned against the unlearned, but it includes its fictional narrator, by implication, on the losing side.

341 **Seinte Frideswide** local female saint reputed to cure the sick and drive out demons

342 **woot** knows

347 **lewed** ignorant

348 **That noght but oonly his bileve kan** who knows nothing but his Creed

351 **what ther sholde bifalle** what was going to happen

352 **marle-pit** clay pit

354 **Me reweth soore of** I am very sorry for

355 **rated** reproved

357 **underspore** lever upwards

362 **haspe** latch
haaf heaved

LINES 365–417   **Nicholas comes to and tells John to make ready for a second flood**

Nicholas stayed stock still, staring into the air. John shook him, shouted at him, and said various prayers over him until Nicholas finally began to sigh and exclaim about the end of the world. Finally coming to his senses, he asked for a drink and promised to tell a secret. John went downstairs and fetched a quart of ale which they shared before Nicholas shut the door and sat down beside him. He swore John to secrecy and told him that he had heard directly from Christ that the following Monday night a great rain would fall, twice as great as Noah's Flood, and drown all mankind in an hour. John's first thought was how he might save Alison.

Nicholas is portrayed as a consummate actor in all the details of this passage, particularly his timing (see Extended Commentaries, Text 2). This is set against John's laughable concoction of prayers, which he reveals make up the religious belief of the working man. It involves a Cross Spell against being possessed by fairies, a children's bedtime prayer, calling on the four evangelists, Matthew, Mark, Luke and John, to bless the four corners of the house. He solemnly says this five times, once facing each wall then once at the door. The 'white paternoster' survives in various forms, all of which are versions of a children's bedtime prayer, deriving from the belief in 'white', as against 'black', magic. The prayer exposes John's faith as superstitious and childish. He calls upon Christ, Saint Benedict and Saint Peter's sister in one charm, and utters another charm against nightmares. The whole is a dramatised exposure of ignorant superstitious piety, functional to the plot but also broadly **satirising** the religious beliefs and education of the urban petit bourgeoisie (see Themes, on Social Climbing). Nicholas's first words reveal another level of innuendo as he promises to tell in privacy a 'thing' which touches them both: 'thing' might be another **euphemism** for a woman's private parts. Despite his earlier pronouncements, John is soon sworn to secrecy by Nicholas when offered access to God's secrets himself. He protests that he is no garrulous gossip, though by now we are getting used to his voice holding forth at length on a range of topics (see Language & Style). Nicholas threatens him that if he does tell anyone he will go mad. This is again **proleptic** as, when John falls from the roof and tells his tale, all his neighbours do indeed believe him to be mad (lines 732–9). Despite his development as a character both gullible and opinionated, his spontaneous concern for his wife maintains the delicate balance between sympathy and ridicule which keeps us interested in his fate.

366 **wende** believed
367 **hente** seized

368 **spitously** fiercely

370 **Cristes passioun** the Crucifixion and Resurrection of Christ

371 **crouche** make a sign of the cross over

wightes beings (here implying supernatural beings)

372 **night-spel** prayer against nightmares

377 **pater-noster** Our Father

380 **sik soore** sigh sorrowfully

381 **eftsoones** so soon

383 **swinke** labour

395 **thou shalt this conseil wreye** you will betray this confidence

397 **forlore** utterly lost

401 **labbe** blabbermouth

402 **lief to gabbe** fond of gossiping

404 **by him that harwed helle** by Christ, who, according to the **apocryphal** Gospel of Nichodemus, rescued all the Old Testament prophets and patriarchs from Hell when he was crucified

408 **quarter night** nine o'clock

LINES 418–92 Nicholas reveals his plan for surviving the flood

Nicholas assured John that all would be well if they used their brains. John admitted that he dimly recollected the story of Noah. Nicholas reminded him that Noah's wife was a legendary scold whom it was difficult to persuade on to the ark. In view of that, John would improve on Noah's plan and provide Nicholas, Alison and himself with individual 'arks', by provisioning three large wooden kneading-troughs or fermentation buckets, and stringing them up in the rafters. John was assured that only the three of them would live, but Nicholas would not say why for fear of revealing too many of God's secrets; Gill the maid and Robin the servant were to be consigned to the flood without protest from John. The troughs were to be provided with an axe so that at the right moment the three fortunate survivors could sever the ropes and cut their way out through the gable of the house on the garden side above the stable. From there they would float out on the waters, joyfully hailing each other to keep their spirits up. The night on which they were to go to bed in the troughs they would have to keep very quiet, however, and John and Alison would have to hang far apart to avoid lascivious looks, as well as deeds which might make them unworthy of being saved.

The pleasure of Nicholas's exposition of his fantasy about the Flood has many sources. Throughout it has a laughably credulous audience in the form of John, who can barely remember the Noah story, and will later confuse Noah with Noel (line 725). The suggested equation of John and Alison with the popular depiction of 600-year-old Noah and his shrewish wife further underscores the stereotypical nature of John and Alison's marriage (see Themes). It also transports the audience yet again into the world of urban festivity and mystery plays in which the actor playing Noah was frequently given a diatribe on the misery of marriage, and Noah's wife, far from being portrayed by a sexy young woman like Alison was probably played by a female impersonator rather like Absolon. Underlying it is a theological joke depending on the **irony** that God sent the original Flood which Noah survived to cleanse the world of lechery, whereas Nicholas's flood is devised as a specific opportunity to indulge his own lechery. The original Noah was also reputed to be an astrologer. But above all it is the dramatic elaboration of Nicholas's account that gives the passage its comic impetus. He blinds John with science, citing learned authorities such as Solomon, plays to his bourgeois avarice by slipping in the reminder that after the Flood they will be lords of all the world, and lovingly sketches in every last detail of the Flood's progress. The storing of picnics in the troughs in case the occupants get peckish awaiting salvation, the precise route of exit from the house, and the image of John and Alison paddling around like farmyard ducks while he calls out to them are all described. The juxtaposition of the mythic story of Noah with petit-bourgeois details about kitchen containers, axes, gable walls and gardens contributes to the Tale's **satirical** undercutting of middle-class pretensions (see Themes, on Social Climbing).

419 **loore and reed** counsel and advice
428 **lorn** lost
429 **yoore** long time
433 **levere** rather

434 **wetheres blake** black sheep

436 **woostou** do you know

440 **kymelin** large flattish wooden tub in which ale was fermented

443 **vitaille** food

445 **aslake** subside

454 **heer-aboute** with all this

458 **purveiaunce** provision (in the sense of foresight as well as literal provisions)

461 **smite the corde atwo** cut the rope in half

476 **ilke** same

480 **Goddes owene heeste deere** God's personal instruction

481 **fer atwinne** far apart

LINES 493–548   **John carries out the plan, and Alison and Nicholas go to bed**

John went off, troubled by the news, and told his secret to Alison, who knew already, of course, but managed to pretend she was scared. John got carried away by his own imagination of Alison drowning, and worked himself into a state. He rushed around assembling all that was needed. He acquired the tubs and hung them in the roof, put bread, cheese and ale into each one, and made the ladders himself. He sent Gill and Robin off to London and, come Monday night, shut the door and lit no candles. They all climbed up into their tubs and stayed still for a while. John was so tired from his exertions that, as soon as he had said his prayers, he fell asleep and snored because his head lay awkwardly. Then Nicholas and Alison went down their ladders and into John's bed, where they had fun.

When Alison hears John's news, she is, the reader is aware, no more innocent in respect of this 'privity' than she is in respect of her own. More domestic details follow, as John buys three different kinds of tub, chooses the picnic, and remembers they need ladders. It is a particularly touching **irony** that John uses the skills of his own trade as a carpenter to construct the means to his cuckolding and later injury. Despite Nicholas's initial suggestion that he and John will contrive the survival of the household together, it becomes clear that Nicholas has provided the brains and now John is expected to supply all the brawn. His concern for Alison is such that it provides the narrator with the opportunity to insert an **apostrophe** on the subject of the power of imagination. Ostensibly this refers to John's neurotic gullibility, by which he sees his beloved wife drowning, but there is surely an **ironic subtext** as the true artificer, Chaucer, pauses to admire the elaborate plot he has constructed, complete with its own ropes and ladders, as it reaches its climax. Chaucer will be more successful as an artificer than Nicholas. The moment when the three are safely installed in their tubs might have evoked, in comic contrast, in the mind's eye of Chaucer's original audience, the popular tragic legend of Saint Nicholas who rescued three children from death in pickling tubs. As Nicholas and Alison steal off to bed they again 'make melody' (see lines 197–8), this time without a musical instrument. Time is measured throughout the course of events by the pealing of bells and the friars' singing of the offices that mark the passage of the day, a counterpoint to the different melody of the young lovers, and the cue to reintroduce Absolon into the plot.

497 **queynte cast** strange contrivance (queynte also means female genitalia)

498 **ferde** behaved

503 **affeccioun** emotion

508 **walwinge** surging

514 **in** boarding house

518 **balkes** rafters

529 **furlong way** two- or three-minute walk (a furlong is one eighth of a mile)

530 **Pater-noster, clom** say your prayers then be quiet

535 **for wery bisynesse** because of exhausting activity

537 **corfew-time** lights-out time

538 **travaille of his goost** unease of his spirit

539 **routeth** snored

547 **laudes** early morning service

548 **freres in the chauncel** friars in the choir of the church

LINES 549–78   **Absolon believes John to be out of town and prepares to woo Alison**

Absolon was out of town at Oseney and happened to ask a monk there about John. The monk said he had not seen the carpenter at work there since Saturday, thought the abbot must have sent him for timber and that he had decided to stay for a couple of days at the supplier's farm. Either that or he was at home. Absolon had seen no sign of him at home, so, concluding that he was away, deduced it was a good time to visit Alison and tell her of his love. He planned to go at dawn to her window for a kiss. He took a nap to get ready.

Absolon's trip to Oseney, though it contributes to the main plot by filling in details of John's working life, also gives Chaucer the opportunity to sketch in another little character portrait of a monk who is even slower-witted than John. In response to a simple question about John's whereabouts, he speculates at length before admitting that he does not know. Absolon chooses to believe what it suits him to believe, which is that John has had to go away to the abbey's estate five miles from Oseney in order to select timber. The job and the distance would involve an overnight stay, as, with fourteenth-century road conditions, a loaded waggon travelled only three to seven miles in a day. The casual revelation that John was absent from work on Oseney Abbey adds a further dimension to the **irony** of the situation. Noah's ark was seen by many learned commentators in the Middle Ages as a **figure** of the church in which the faithful weathered the deluge of sin in the world. As a church carpenter, John is a true Noah who has been distracted from useful pious works by the lovers' trick. Absolon now lays his own plans carefully, thinking of the low window and suffering an itchy mouth. He believes that this presages a kiss at least – he cannot bring himself to consider what more he might achieve. He will, of course, later receive his kiss which will make his mouth itch more than he anticipates (lines 626–31). Unlike the true **courtly lover** who wastes away from lack of sleep when in love (see Themes, on Love), he takes an expedient nap so as to face his love-making fresh.

552 **disporte** relax
553 **axed upon cas a cloisterer** asked by chance a regular monk
560 **grange** estate farm
565 **sikirly** truly
573 **parfay** by my faith

LINES 579–621   Absolon goes wooing and Alison is persuaded into a
kiss

Absolon got up at dawn, dressed neatly and chewed breath-freshening
herbs. He went to John's house and stood at the hinged window which
was so low it came down to chest-height. He coughed discreetly and
called out endearments to Alison. Annoyed at being disturbed, she told
him sharply to go away or she would throw a stone. He protested and
they began to bargain. Eventually he promised he would go away if
she let him kiss her first. She agreed, and promised Nicholas a good
laugh.

Absolon's preparations for his wooing adventure connect both
with what preceded them and what is to come (see Extended
Commentaries – Text 3). His absurd and elaborate precautions
against bad breath, using cardamom, licorice and other herbs,
remind us of his dislike of bodily smells, and Chaucer also exploits
the Middle English pun on 'likerous', which means both 'lecherous',
which Nicholas and Alison are, and licorice, which Absolon chews.
The sweet perfumes and much of the tone of his love-making
provide a **parodic** echo of the Bible's most famous love song,
Song of Solomon, which was commonly interpreted as God's song
of love for his people. The adoption of such a high **register**,
implying mystical love, is another source of humour in such an
incongruously carnal and domestic context. Absolon complains of
many of the symptoms that afflict the **courtly lover** – sickness and
loss of appetite – again humorously undercut by the **imagery** which
makes him a lot less attractive as he describes uncontrollable
sweating and bleating like a lamb after its mother's teat, or a turtle
dove. He says he is unable to eat more than a girl can, thus
completing a string of images which undermine his virility. The
following exchange adds tonal incongruity as Alison meets his love
plaint by calling him a fool and threatening to throw a stone at him.
This may be, as some commentators have suggested, an **ironic**
reference to the biblical punishment of stoning to death which was
meted out both for adultery and for blasphemy such as Absolon's if
he really is using biblical verses in his wooing. More immediately,
however, Alison's threat works as a cold blast of the everyday,

treating Absolon as if he were a cat howling under her window and keeping her awake. Where she might find a stone in her bedroom is not really worth the speculation it has caused. She says that of course she loves another, as a married woman would, were it not that the reader knows that she is cynically referring to Nicholas who is currently in bed with her. The kiss, Absolon hopes, will be the first of many as he kneels to receive it, although she presents it simply as a bargain to get rid of him and promises Nicholas a laugh.

582 **greyn** grain (cardamom)

584 **trewe-love** four-leaved lucky herb paris

585 **wende** believed

588 **raughte** reached

589 **semy soun** slight sound

595 **swelte** melt

601 **'com pa me'** come-kiss-me

605 **a twenty devel wey** in the name of twenty devils

610 **go thy wey therwith** be on your way with that

616 **at alle degrees** in all respects

618 **oore** grace

620 **com of** hurry up

LINES 622–51   **Absolon kisses Alison's bare backside in the dark**

The night was very dark. Absolon wiped his mouth as Alison put her bare backside out of the window. He kissed her lingeringly before he realised what was happening, then jumped back, aware that he had kissed something hairy, and knowing women do not have beards. Alison slammed the window shut and she and Nicholas had a good laugh at Absolon's expense. He went off, rubbing his mouth with anything he could lay hands on, completely cured of his love, and swearing to get even.

See Extended Commentaries, Text 3.

627 **savourly** with relish

639 **froteth** scrubbed

640 **chippes** wood-shavings

642 **bitake** entrust

Sathanas Satan

643 **levere** rather

644 **Of this despit awroken for to be** to avenge this humiliation

645 **I ne hadde ybleynt** I wish I had not been deceived

646 **yqueynt** quenched

651 **ybete** beaten

LINES 652–81   **Absolon plans his revenge at the blacksmith's shop and returns to Alison**

Absolon went quietly over the street to Gervase at the smithy. Gervase wondered what was the matter and put it down to girl trouble, but Absolon would not be drawn and merely asked him if he could borrow a red-hot coulter, part of the plough that Gervase was forging, refusing to say what he wanted it for. He went back to the window, coughed and knocked again.

> After having a good cry, Absolon decides to get even. He commends his soul to Satan, so eager for revenge that he is prepared to enter into a pact with the devil. 'Hell', however, turns out to be the smithy over the road belonging to genial local smith Gervase, who is engaged in forging the parts of a plough. Smithies were associated with hell in medieval art, for the obvious reason that they were dirty black places full of fire and smoke, as well as because of their association with the Norse God Vulcan. Absolon's resort to such a cosy 'hell' further undercuts the high seriousness with which he takes the events of his wooing. Gervase seems to find nothing odd about being burst in upon by a local young man who is out chasing girls in the middle of the night and greets Absolon with the easy familiarity of one man of the world to another. Absolon armed with the iron disk of the coulter, the plough's cutting blade, turns from **parodic courtly lover** to parodic jousting knight, returning to the scene of his humiliation to issue a challenge. Critics have variously found in this episode phallic **imagery** attaching to the plough, certainly conventional by Shakespeare's time, and a possible **ironic** inversion of the biblical instruction to turn swords into ploughshares (Isaiah 2:4).

652 **A softe paas** walking quietly

655 **shaar** ploughshare

656 **esily** gently

659 **for Cristes sweete tree** by Christ's Cross

662 **upon the viritoot** ?on the trot

663 **Seinte Note** Saint Neot (who according to legend saved King Alfred during a night's wooing)

664 **roghte** cared

666 **moore tow on his distaf** more on his plate

     tow flax

     distaf spinning implement

672 **poke** pouch

LINES 682–707   Nicholas farts in Absolon's face; Absolon burns Nicholas's backside

When Alison answered, Absolon said he had brought her a gold ring which he would exchange for another kiss. Nicholas had got up for a piss, and thought he would get Absolon to kiss him, so he opened the window and stuck his backside right out. Absolon asked Alison to speak because he couldn't see where she was, and Nicholas farted in his face so fiercely that he was nearly blinded. But Absolon was ready, and thrust the hot iron into Nicholas's backside, causing a weal as big as a hand. It hurt so much that Nicholas thought he would die. He cried out for water.

Absolon again plays on Alison's weakness for presents of monetary value, offering her an engraved gold ring which belonged to his mother. It is at this point that Nicholas makes his fatal error. So conceited is he at how well all his plans have come off, that he attempts to repeat a trick. A mundane detail which further reduces the romantic status of events tells us that Nicholas has already got out of bed to make water; water which he will shortly be crying out for. The rhyme of 'kiss' with 'piss' epitomises Chaucer's comic technique here by sharply juxtaposing Absolon's romantic pretensions with everyday physical reality. Nicholas rewards Absolon's squeamishness by farting in his face. The fart may also be taken to stand for all the hot air which has gone into Nicholas's plans. Chaucer uses a fart symbolically in this way in another fabliau (see Literary Background, on Fabliau), *The Summoner's Tale*, where the division of a fart into twelve equal pieces becomes the object of an ingeniously solved arithmetical puzzle. One way of getting rid of demons was said to be to fart in their faces or to throw fecal matter at them: Nicholas and Alison could be purging their night of love of Absolon's demonic intrusions. Absolon's thrusting of the hot iron up Nicholas's backside, on the other hand, has been read as a symbolic act of sodomy, given Absolon's effeminate nature. On the other hand, Absolon as a surgeon would have been well-practised at cauterisation, the sealing of a wound by burning, and cauterisation in the anus was a common surgical practice at the time. Nicholas's cry for water after Absolon has applied the red-hot iron to his backside acts as the punchline to the whole narrative, as it brings the whole edifice of the plot **metaphorically** and literally crashing down all at once.

688 **ygrave** engraved
691 **amenden al the jape** improve upon the trick
697 **I noot nat** I don't know
699 **thonder-dent** clap of thunder
700 **yblent** blinded
704 **toute** buttocks

LINES 708–46   **John thinks the Flood has come, endures a fall; all the neighbours come to laugh, and so the Tale ends**

John awoke at Nicholas's cry and, thinking the Flood had come, cut the ropes with his axe and plummeted to the floor where he lay unconscious. Alison and Nicholas ran into the street for help, and all the neighbours came to stare at John who had broken his arm. He was determined to tell them what had happened, but, as soon as he tried, Nicholas and Alison shouted him down and told everyone that he was mad and had hung three tubs in the roof because he had a fantasy about the Flood. They said that they had been humouring him. All the neighbours laughed at him, gaped at the roof, and would not listen to him. Thus Nicholas made love to the carpenter's wife, despite her husband's vigilance. Thus Absolon kissed her private parts, and thus Nicholas got a burnt backside. That is the end, God save us all!

Whether John's confusion of Noah with Noel is symptomatic of his general intellectual capacities or of his befuddled sleepy state matters little, for the whole edifice of his belief is about to collapse. **Ironically** it is the axe, one of the tools of his trade, that brings about his injury. The introduction of the audience of neighbours at this point both reminds the reader of the close proximity, and lack of privacy of any kind in a small town, It also provides Chaucer with an opportunity to retell the sequence of events in summary. The garrulous John had earlier promised that he was not a gossip (line 401) and now no-one will listen to him. The end of the Tale suggests that all town-dwellers are hungry for defamatory information about their neighbours in a society where everyone knows everyone else's business. The exposure of the lovers to John, and of John to his neighbours, takes place just as day breaks and common sense is restored, with a blessing on all the characters and the pilgrims in the audience. The Tale begins and ends with assertions that characters are suffering from fantasies, which may be taken as an indication that the reader should not try to take any of it too seriously at all.

712 **smoot** struck

713 **he foond neither to selle** he did not stop to negotiate

714 **celle** floor

715 **aswowne** unconscious

719 **gauren** stare

721 **brosten** broken

723 **he was anon bore doun** he was straight away overruled

733 **kiken** gazed

    cape gaped

742 **swived** fucked

744 **nether ye** rear eye

PART THREE

CRITICAL APPROACHES

CHARACTERISATION

In a layered narrative like *The Canterbury Tales*, characterisation is a complex matter. Characters within *The Miller's Tale* fulfil the functions required of them by the plot and, as with any story in which the participants are going to be the objects of ridicule, they are animated just enough to appear plausible, but do not develop the kind of complex inner life which would cause the audience to sympathise with them too much.

The complications arise, however, when we consider who is the creator of Alison, Nicholas, Absolon and John, for the Miller is a fictional character too. He exists in a different layer in the narrative composition, but is given physical characteristics both in *The General Prologue* and in the introduction to his Tale. It is Chaucer's creation of the Miller's voice to which we are supposed to be listening. But Chaucer himself is part of the fiction, for he has put himself on the pilgrimage, and pretends that the retelling of each story is a prodigious feat of memory. In a modern novel, the inner thoughts of characters can provide the reader with a lens through which to see the world the character inhabits; in *The Miller's Tale* understanding the function of character is about being alert to a series of lenses through which we are offered a picture of life in medieval Oxford.

THE MILLER

The Miller is an ugly thug who can break down doors with his head. Critics have argued that details of his appearance draw on the medieval science of physiognomy, connecting physical appearance with astrological influences which in turn were thought to govern character. His wide nostrils and mouth, for example, suggest lechery and gluttony, whereas his red hair indicates a choleric temper governed by the planet Mars. The comparison of his open mouth to a furnace reinforces this reading, while also suggesting the entrance to hell, invariably depicted as a mouth. Commentators have been unable to agree on whether his features combine to make him look most like a pig, an ape or a gargoyle. He is armed to the teeth, and he uses what brains he has chiefly to cheat his clients. His leisure pursuits are competition wrestling and playing the bagpipe, a musical instrument pictured in comic medieval illustrations of drunken revelry as well as caricatures of devils in hell (*The General Prologue*, lines 547–68). He may seem to be one of the least genteel pilgrims in *The Canterbury Tales*, but like all his companions he has the leisure and money to go on a pilgrimage.

  The medieval miller was an important man in the village community. He might run a windmill or a watermill, but as his mill would be owned by the lord of the manor, its use would be compulsory for all the lord's tenants. Everyone from peasant to farmer had to take their grain to him for grinding. He was paid by the retention of his 'toll' or percentage of the flour. Like Chaucer's pilgrim Reeve – a bailiff or overseer of the manor – with whom the Miller falls into dispute, he has many opportunities for making his way in the world by cheating lord and peasant alike.

  The Miller is not supposed to tell his Tale when he does at all. But he is drunk, belligerent, noisy, and claims to have something to tell which follows on neatly from *The Knight's Tale* (lines 17–19). As he explains that his Tale too is about the rivalry of two men over one woman, he reveals his philosophy of life: all women are treacherous, sexually rampant creatures, so most husbands are cuckolds and it is best not to enquire too deeply into such matters (lines 42–58). He is unstoppable, so the Host gives way to him. The Tale which follows, although drawn straight from the social world and preoccupations of the Miller, is an implausibly clever and orderly affair.

CHAUCER THE VENTRILOQUIST

At the end of the Miller's *Prologue*, the voice of Chaucer intervenes, asking his audience not to judge him on the content of *The Miller's Tale* which, because of his project, he now must repeat (lines 59–78). The sensitive reader is advised to choose another Tale, since *The Canterbury Tales* as a whole contain something for everyone, and no-one should, in any case, take a bit of fun too seriously. Yet the reader knows that this lewd drunken oaf, who is about to offend finer feelings, is, just like the pilgrimage itself, another invention of Chaucer's. Chaucer's characterisation of himself is the complicating factor which prevents the pilgrims in *The Canterbury Tales* from being read like characters in a play. Chaucer puts himself on the pilgrimage, and will later attempt twice to tell stories in his own voice with disastrous results – *Melibee* and *Sir Thopas* are both experiments in bad story-telling. The whole, completely fictitious retelling of the pilgrims' stories is presented as a diligent feat of memory on Chaucer's part. His caricature of himself as a timid and inept inventor of stories allows him to suggest that he is not competent to sift the good from the bad in what he heard, so he must retell it all. From this position he is able to tell a raunchy story about illicit sex in downtown Oxford by hiding behind the character of a drunken miller. Chaucer implies that he cannot control the Miller any more than the Host can, and the Miller, being drunk, cannot control himself. Thus Chaucer uses the character of the Miller to give himself the freedom to tell a Tale about sex. But equally he does not let the Miller's drunkenness and limited intelligence constrain him from creating a story whose narrative structure and rhymed verse are well beyond any capabilities the Miller, who himself admits that he is slurring his words (lines 30–32), could possibly have.

CHARACTERS IN THE TALE

Just as the characters of the Canterbury pilgrims in *The General Prologue* are categorised by their station in life, so too the characters in *The Miller's Tale* are socially nuanced. The presentation of John fuels the friction between the Miller and the Reeve – also a carpenter by trade – (lines 36–41) by suggesting that all carpenters are ill-educated, complacent and superstitious. Absolon's assorted and mediocre accomplishments (lines 218–28) represent the parochiality of all small-town life in the way that a London court audience, such as Chaucer was writing for, would perceive it. Nicholas, the ubiquitous student lodger, is too clever for his own good. Yet he is the hero of the Tale, something which has led some critics to suggest that he is Chaucer's surrogate, representing the triumph of intelligence over pretentiousness and money. Delicious Alison, good enough for any farmer to marry, and any Lord to bed (lines 161–2), is available as the male reader's sexual fantasy.

John and Alison, Nicholas and Absolon all develop distinctive and memorable identities in the course of *The Miller's Tale*, but they have little psychological reality beyond the functions they fulfil in illustrating the social groups at which Chaucer is poking fun (see Themes, on Social Climbing) and in bringing the plot to its conclusion (see Narrative Techniques). Each is a collection of characteristics, and each is appropriately rewarded: John is superstitious and guards his wife too closely, so he ends up with a broken arm, and as the laughing-stock of his small social world (lines 718–34); Nicholas is both sexually precocious and too clever for his own good, so he has his backside burnt (lines 701–7); Absolon is fastidious and hates bad smells so his quite unrealistic adulterous ambitions are rewarded with a fart in the face (lines 698–700). And if Alison appears to get away unpunished, the reader is still aware that all her liveliness will once more be contained within the affluent prison of her marriage.

THEMES

FORETELLING THE FUTURE

The Miller's Tale contains within it a thematic discussion of the relative merits of accepting your God-given lot in life as against succumbing to the temptations of trying to predict the future. It is unfashionable now to overmoralise the Tale, which becomes tempting as soon as serious themes are identified; modern criticism rather favours a festive reading (see Critical History). Nonetheless, the Tale contains an amount of religious commentary about the advantages and disadvantages of being able to look ahead. Nicholas is not content with using science to predict the future by studying the stars; he uses his reputation as an astronomer to manufacture his own future and to bring about his unforeseen downfall. John, on the other hand, first presents himself as a pious ignoramus and proud of it, but is soon converted to the advantages of prediction when he is promised that it can save his life. His conversion to the science of prediction earns him a broken arm and public humiliation. What prevents the theme from becoming too ponderously moral is its constant undercutting by references to the immediate, the everyday and the physical.

The Miller warns in his Prologue that men should not pry into their wives' private matters, let alone God's (line 55–6). Wives, like God, are inscrutable, dangerous and unpredictable. John's view that the physical world is difficult and dangerous enough without examining the metaphysical is similar. He tells the tale of the man who by looking too much at the stars fell into a pit (lines 351–2). The question is not really one of the inscrutability of God and the danger of violating it, so much as the down-to-earth message never to mind God's inscrutability when the unpredictability of everyday things, like wives and deep holes, provides a more immediate cause for anxiety.

SOCIAL CLIMBING

The outcome of *The Miller's Tale* is a fall from grace for everyone concerned in the story, and 'falling' is a thematically charged concept. At the level of plot, the characters fall because of their overambitious sexual aspirations, but thematically the fall is one into humiliation for a group of characters who are exposed as social climbers. If the Tale operates at a moral level at all, the moral that it has to offer is a social one.

Labour shortages meant that there were many opportunities for survivors of the Black Death to advance themselves socially and to amass wealth, especially in the towns (see Historical Background). Social distinctions remained marked, however, between wealth accruing from landownership, and riches amassed from trade. As Chaucer wrote primarily for the cultured landed classes surrounding the royal court, there were many opportunities for poking fun at the social climbing of the new arrivals in the middle class.

John is wealthy. He has a large modern house, probably in the suburbs, and has managed to attract a pretty young wife – or more probably her father. He has the confidence and complacency that comes with wealth and is quick to offer advice, but his advice betrays his humble origins by showing that he is effectively uneducated. He admires ignorance (line 347). He also supplements his income by taking in lodgers, which is not something a member of the upper classes would do. He is completely taken in by Nicholas's trick because he seems to be rather in awe of learning and cannot tell a lazy lecherous student from a true scholar.

Alison his wife is dressed in a way that shows both that she is wealthy and that she is unaccustomed to wealth (see Extended Commentaries, Text 1). Her costume is immodest and vulgarly fashionable. Her brooch is too large (lines 157–8), and she wears her purse, decorated with brass where a lady would have gold, in a rather obvious way (line 143). She is even compared to a coin herself, though one of only middling value (line 148). Her value in the eyes of the landed classes is precisely articulated: because she is pretty a lord might take her to bed, but no-one above the rank of yeoman farmer would consider marrying her (line 162).

Absolon too is precisely placed amongst the small-town middle classes. As a barber he is fundamentally of the same trading class as John, but as John climbs socially by a display of money, Absolon's social pretensions relate to his attempts to appear cultivated. As a parish clerk he would have a rudimentary education, but not one approaching the university education which Nicholas is at least notionally receiving. His accomplishments are clerical, as he can draw up deeds of transaction according to set formulae. The precision of his appearance, and his mastery of two musical instruments, suggest a strenuous effort to appear refined, which is undercut by the narrator's view that his dancing is good but only by Oxford standards.

Much of the Tale's humour depends upon an understanding of the consensus snob values of Chaucer and his social group. These are complex because they involve educational and geographical snobbery as well as social discrimination. The provincial nature of all the action, and particularly the focus on Absolon as a big fish in a small pond, is designed to appeal to the London-based audience. This audience would not be Londoners by birth, but aristocrats from country estates who gravitated to London as the cultural centre of the royal court at Westminster. This audience would not be graduates any more than Chaucer was, but their wide experience of the kind of culture acquired from manuscript acquisition and reading only available to the leisured classes would put them in a position to look down at the ignorance displayed particularly by John. Social discrimination is indicated through a number of the details mentioned above but is also inherent in the contrast the Tale offers between the two narrative **genres** of **fabliau** and **Romance** (see Literary Background).

LOVE

True love is hard to find in *The Miller's Tale*, unless the sentimental reader chooses to believe that John really loves his wife. Chaucer weaves a web of **irony** around contrasting types of relationships between the sexes. '**Courtly love**' is the term used to describe the conventional refined behaviour of aristocratic lovers in high chivalric **Romance**. Chaucer uses the conventions of courtly love here as part of his strategy for showing up the social pretensions of the lovers. In high Romance it is a mark of the lovers' refinement that the lady remains unattainably chaste while her would-be suitor composes songs for her, keeps his love secret to protect her reputation, becomes unable to eat or sleep and is in danger of death if she will not accept him. Acceptance means allowing him to declare himself and to offer her his service.

In *The Miller's Tale*, both Nicholas and Absolon behave like courtly lovers in different ways. Nicholas uses the language of courtly love the first time he encounters Alison alone, and she reciprocates by being shocked and outraged by his approach. He claims that he will die of secret love (line 170). The circumstances of the encounter, however, make plain that Nicholas's ambitions, far from being refined, are sexual. The language is full of possible sexual meanings too (see Narrative Techniques, on Diction), and all the while he is wooing her he is touching her in ways that would be quite unthinkable in high Romance.

Absolon's relationship with courtly love is a different one, for he believes that wooing should be done by the book. He has no notion of the realities of sex, and his extreme fastidiousness about bodily odours suggests that he would be unlikely to cope. For Absolon, love *is* high Romance, and when he falls in love he goes to Alison's house at night to sing love songs derived from the Song of Solomon (Old Testament) under her window. He is, like the courtly lover, ennobled by love, so that he generously refuses to take the collection in church (lines 242–3). His tragedy, and our joke, is that he cannot tell the difference between story books and reality. He chooses the wrong object for his desires, one who shares a bedroom with her husband, and one who meets his wooing not with a modest rebuttal but the threat of throwing a stone (line 604).

It could be argued that sexuality is a theme in the Tale, but without the **parodic** contrast with other literary types of love, sexuality would

remain no more than a device to drive the plot forward. It is the contrast
between different types of love which elevates love to thematic status.

LANGUAGE & STYLE

IMAGERY

Imagery provides Chaucer with his opportunities for suggesting parallels
which make the texture of *The Miller's Tale* more dense. Many of the
major fields of imagery in the Tale are established in the description
of Alison (see Extended Commentaries, Text 1), all of them working
towards portraying her as attractive but away from suggesting that there
is anything refined about her. Imagery associated with Absolon then
offers variants on that established for Alison, drawing on it to make him
seem both foolish and effeminate.

The first consists of comparisons with animals: she is slim as a
weasel (line 126), soft as sheep's wool (line 141), noisy as a swallow (line
150), frisky as a kid or calf (line 152). The prevalence of young animals is
attractive, although there are less attractive undertones suggested by the
image of a weasel which is a vicious thief and the swallow which was
noted for its lechery in medieval animal lore. The other animal references
take the reader into the world of the farmyard, which removes any
suggestion of courtly refinement. Farmyard animal imagery occurs
elsewhere in the Tale, in, for example, Nicholas's fantasy, for John's
benefit, about the three lucky Flood survivors who will row around in
their kneading troughs, Alison following John like a duck after a drake
(line 468). There is one real animal in the Tale, the cat with which
Nicholas has some affinity as it chooses to come and go from his room by
stealth (line 333). Absolon has a fantasy that he is a cat and Alison a
mouse (lines 238–9), but fails to recognise that she is no mouse, but a
weasel, and weasels eat mice. His eyes are compared to a goose (line 209),
though he sings like a nightingale (line 269), pines like a dove or like a
lamb looking for its mother's teat (lines 596–8). None of these is an
image of virility.

Alison is also compared to a number of fruits and common flowers,
reinforcing the domestic range of the field of imagery. Her eyebrows are
black as sloes (line 138), she is prettier than an early-opening pear-tree

(line 140), and her breath smells of apples (line 154). She is not a rose, like the classic courtly lady, nor a lily, like the Virgin Mary, but pretty as an English hedgerow, like a primrose or other small wild flower. Add to that her apron like milk, her mouth sweet as ale or mead, and what emerges is a range of images of food and abundance which can be associated with sexuality. Absolon on the other hand, unable to eat more than a maid (line 599), is associated with sweet-smelling herbs which he chews to improve his breath (lines 582–4), and sends Alison sweet wine and mead as presents (line 270). He compares her to cinnamon and honey (lines 590–1). Olfactory imagery in the form of an array of sweet smells associated with both Alison and Absolon is built up through the tale in preparation for the fart with which Absolon is rewarded for his fastidious courtship.

The range of images most obviously associated with the characters emphasises their provinciality, but they are also representatives of the small-town middle classes. Hence money also forms an important field of imagery. Again it begins in the description of Alison who not only carries her purse ostentatiously (lines 142–3), but is like a newly forged noble (line 148), a coin worth six shillings and eight pence, or one third of a pound, not a value great enough to imply a real compliment. Absolon later betrays that he belongs to that same world, when his one gesture of magnanimity is a refusal to take the church collection, and when he offers Alison money as a love token (line 272). Nicholas, on the other hand, is a poor student who has already discovered that, fortunately, her favours come free of charge.

Like smells, music and melody also provide a range of images associated with sex. Alison's shrill swallow's voice associates her with lechery, whereas both her suitors are musicians and singers. Nicholas's singing **parodies** the angel Gabriel wooing the Virgin Mary (line 108), whereas Absolon's nighttime voice is compared to the nightingale's, traditionally a female image associated with lost love. Images associated with Absolon and John are often in a context where they are substitutes for the real thing, whereas associated with Nicholas and Alison the image is a **metaphor** for the real thing. Nicholas plays his psaltery when he has successfully got Alison to agree to sleep with him when the opportunity presents itself (lines 197–8), and when the opportunity does arise (line 544) they 'make melody' together.

Speech

John the carpenter is given dramatic character, less through obvious imagery than through the construction of a plausible voice. His speech is particularly characterised by tedious platitudes which state the blindingly obvious, such as no-one knows when death will strike (lines 341–2) or no-one knows what will happen to him (line 342). These instantly mark John out as slow-witted. His speech is littered with commonplace pieties, prayers and exclamations about God and the saints, which expose his version of religion as little more than unthinking superstition. When involved in a conversation he is soon out of his depth and can barely recall the story of Noah's Flood (line 429). John is proud of his lack of education, and blesses the ignorant man (line 347), yet is also very complacent, demonstrating with the help of cautionary tales that he understands the ways of the world better than Nicholas (lines 350–2). It is precisely this combination of complacency and limited intellect that makes both his marriage and his later gullibility plausible. He also sounds distinctly like the Miller (lines 43–58).

The construction of Nicholas's voice too, rather than revealing a fully rounded character, serves to lend texture and support to the plot. Nicholas's undoing arises not because he is lecherous but because he is too clever by half. This is anticipated in the long piece of direct speech during which he describes the preparation and likely outcome of the 'Flood' to John (lines 405–90). It is full of questioning, cajoling and other devices to keep John interested, but it also swiftly moves off into the realms of delicious fantasy as Nicholas imagines the three of them floating around on the waters in their kneading-tubs, calling out to one another. In other words he gets carried away by his own invention. It is when he gets carried away with the cleverness of another trick, the one played on Absolon, and cannot resist repeating it, that he gets burnt.

Alison's voice is rarely heard, although it is described as loud and shrill (line 149), like the shrieking of a swallow. When we do hear her in direct speech, she is almost always in the expletive, either telling Nicholas to get his hands off or else (lines 178–9), or threatening to throw a stone at Absolon (line 604). Alison is not a woman of words but of action.

The Tale also creates the voices of a very dithering monk (lines 556–62) and affable Gervase the blacksmith (lines 661–3, 671–4) who is thrown by nothing. Both of them lend additional texture to the Tale.

NARRATIVE TECHNIQUES

The overall structure of *The Miller's Tale* has been cleverly contrived to mirror *The Knight's Tale* which it follows. It concerns two men in pursuit of one woman, a triangular structure. Relationships and action throughout the Tale take the shape of intersecting triangles. When John is either absent or asleep, Alison and Nicholas play, and when John is at home or awake the action turns to Absolon. When Nicholas explains the coming Flood to John, Alison is excluded, but John immediately runs off and tells her the 'privetee' he has learned from Nicholas, so that the plot hatched first by Nicholas and Alison together proceeds around the triangle and back to where it started. There are no 'meanwhiles' or other devices, but alternation in the location of action seems to occur naturally, without the transitions obviously marking simultaneous action.

The pace of the action is varied and very tightly controlled. Sometimes it moves forward from one thing to another in quick succession, while at others it is deliberately retentive, holding back the next piece of crucial information which will progress the plot to its inevitable end. This is particularly apparent while Nicholas is in his trance. He is busy while John is asleep, but while he is passive it is John's turn to be busy. The account of John's bustling around, commanding Robin, having doors broken down, fetching and carrying quarts of ale, contrasts with Nicholas's carefully orchestrated and slowly timed return to consciousness (see Extended Commentaries, Text 2). John will later be busy again, rushing to and fro acquiring troughs and making a ladder in preparation for the Flood. His final, equally futile burst of activity occurs at lines 712–15 where the audience sees the cord, the axe and the sudden fall. It becomes clear that all John's activity, all the action of his parts of the plot have been wholly futile.

Absolon too engages in bursts of feverish activity, rushing to and fro to Oseney, preparing himself for a would-be date, combing hair, chewing herbs, dressing up, and wandering around with his giterne at night,

worked up into a sweat (line 594). Like John's, his activity is beside the
point and, like John, he finds this level of activity exhausting and has to
take a nap (line 577). Only his final decisive action with the hot iron
coulter achieves any goal.

It is one of the Tale's structural **ironies** that fast-pace physical
action does not move things forward so much as talk does. The real
mover and plotter in *The Miller's Tale* is Nicholas, whose mental
processes achieve more than the bustling of the other two men. His most
decisive actions involve flattering Alison, feigning a catatonic state, then
talking John into believing an improbable story. His only strenuous
physical action takes place in bed with Alison.

The action of *The Miller's Tale* seems to mimic Nicholas's way of
working, setting things up very carefully before making any decisive
moves. Action does not actually commence until line 163, when the
narrative allows two of the characters to interact for the first time. Until
then, most of the telling has been given over to passages of description,
and there is still the long description of Absolon to come. Description
alternates with short passages of action and a relatively large amount of
direct speech to move the Tale forward. The impression that there is
always a lot going on in the narrative is an illusion supported by the
inclusion of lots of concrete detailing in description, talk and action alike.
Pace increases as the Tale progresses, however, until the whole carefully
crafted and tightly controlled verbal edifice comes crashing down,
triggered by Nicholas's cry for water. It is also possible to read the Tale's
structure as a **metaphor** for sex which is its fundamental subject and the
preoccupation of all its characters. It involves a deal of narrative foreplay,
a fantasy climax which places John, Alison and Nicholas in the roof, a
moment of disillusion and a fall, followed by public humiliation for all
involved.

DICTION

The Tale's diction, syntax and rhyme scheme conform to a plain low
style. The dominant sentence structure is **paratactic**, with few **rhetorical**
flourishes. The rhyme scheme consists of **couplets** of **iambic
pentameters**. There are few abstract words. Chaucer does, however,
indulge one literary device which is in keeping with the subject matter,

and that is the use of puns. Language too can deceive. Punning, the technique of exploiting the double meaning of words, is not just the source of the occasional laugh but a structural principle in *The Miller's Tale*. Single words sustain the possibility of double meanings, but the balance of which meaning is uppermost shifts as the story progresses. Certain words with potentially abstract and concrete senses move down from the abstract to the concrete as the pretentiousness of certain characters is stripped away.

Nicholas is associated with the adjective 'hende', which can mean 'courteous', but also simply 'handy'. At first, the ideal neat and clean lodger, he seems to charm both Alison and John by his nice manners, but as it becomes clear that what underlies the attraction between Nicholas and Alison is a mutual need for sex, the reader becomes aware that it is possibly simple physical proximity which is his main attraction. Pushing the reader in this direction, Chaucer alternates 'hende' with 'nie' ('nigh' or 'near') at line 288.

The Miller prefaces his Tale by rather pompously advising the Reeve not to enquire into God's 'privetee' or his wife's. John too has severe doubts about whether God's 'privetee' is out of bounds or not. The word seems initially to mean 'secrets', but it always contains within it the more explicit physical meaning of a woman's 'private parts'. What begins as a discussion of metaphysics, and the rights and wrongs of foretelling the future by prying into God's secrets, soon degenerates into a tale of adultery, as Nicholas merely uses God's 'privetee' as a ploy to get at Alison's.

Similarly, John's fascination with the future arises because he has an anxiety about what will 'falle', that is befall or happen. The answer is that in believing he knows what will 'falle' he is heading for an all too physical fall from his own roof to his own floor. Chaucer signals that he is playing this verbal game in lines 349–53, when he recounts the moral tale of the man who walked around looking at the stars to see what would 'bifalle' and, because he was not looking where he was going, 'was yfalle', that is, fell, into a clay-pit. Chaucer's **irony** is that John here **proleptically** describes himself.

There are other puns throughout the Tale, all holding the possibility of a higher abstract meaning in tension with a physical, often sexual, one. For example, lines 167–8 both end with the word 'queynte', working in exactly the same way as 'privetee' and having a similar range of meaning, from 'sly' or 'subtle' to 'private parts'. And when Nicholas threatens to 'spille' (line 120) if Alison will not accept his love, it is unclear whether he means to dwindle away and perish like a true **courtly lover** or to have an orgasm and wet himself. There is also the half-pun on 'likerous', lecherous or sexy, which is used to describe Alison (line 136), and 'licoris', licorice, which Absolon the unsexy chews (line 582) to make himself more attractive to women. Both words sound the same. Each such pun contains within it in miniature the pattern of the whole Tale's structure, an edifice built on pretentiousness and deceit which will end with a fart, the smell of burnt flesh and a crash to the ground.

EXTENDED COMMENTARIES

TEXT 1 (LINES 125–62)

Fair was this yonge wyf, and therwithal 125
As any wezele hir body gent and smal.
A ceint she werede, barred al of silk,
A barmclooth eek as whit as morne milk
Upon hir lendes, ful of many a goore.
Whit was hir smok, and broiden al bifoore 130
And eek bihinde, on hir coler aboute,
Of col-blak silk, withinne and eek without.
The tapes of hir white voluper
Were of the same suite of hir coler;
Hir filet brood of silk, and set ful hye. 135
And sikerly she hadde a likerous ye;
Ful smale ypulled were hire browes two,
And tho were bent and blake as any sloo.
She was ful moore blisful on to see
Than is the newe pere-jonette tree, 140
And softer than the wolle is of a wether.
And by hir girdel heeng a purs of lether,
Tasseled with silk, and perled with latoun.
In al this world, to seken up and doun,
There nis no man so wys that koude thenche 145
So gay a popelote or swich a wenche.
Ful brighter was the shining of hir hewe
Than in the Tour the noble yforged newe.
But of hir song, it was as loude and yerne
As any swalwe sittinge on a berne. 150
Therto she koude skippe and make game,
As any kide or calf folwinge his dame.
Hir mouth was sweete as bragot or the meeth,
Or hoord of apples leyd in hey or heeth.
Winsinge she was, as is a joly colt, 155

Long as a mast, and upright as a bolt.
A brooch she baar upon hir lowe coler,
As brood as is the boos of a bokeler.
Hir shoes were laced on hir legges hye,
She was a primerole, a piggesnie,   160
For any lord to leggen in his bedde,
Or yet for any good yeman to wedde.

Without warning, Chaucer breaks off from setting up his story to present his readers with a detailed description of Alison, the heroine. Fabliau stories do not usually indulge in passages of pure description of this kind: Chaucer draws upon the practices of Romance narration for this interruption to the action. In Romance such passages are known as *effictio*, and generally anatomise the heroine as a suitable object for the hero's love. Her hair, face, body, clothing, voice, deportment and habits may all be described using metaphors and similes to pay her extravagant compliments. Chaucer's description of Alison conforms to this pattern, but draws its images from untypical areas of life and experience.

The reader already knows that Alison is an eighteen-year-old girl, newly married to an old carpenter who dotes on her (lines 113–15). The passage begins by stating simply that she is pretty, but immediately startles by comparing her slender shape to a weasel (line 126). Weasels are aggressive little animals, and in any case it is not usual to compare beautiful ladies to small carnivores. Not only is she slender, she is not remotely curvaceous but tall as a mast and straight as an arrow (line 156), neither of them particularly feminine images. Alison is presented as a tall strong young woman who can look after herself, anticipating her later behaviour, for she does nothing in the course of the Tale that she does not want to.

In the following lines, Chaucer leaves off describing Alison herself to tell us what she is wearing in great detail. She has a striped silk girdle or belt round her weasel-thin waist. Beneath it, around her hips is an apron or overskirt, white as milk, and made up of lots of gores, or pieces of material (lines 127–9). Immediately the reader is pulled up by another apparently incongruous image: whiteness may be associated with lilies or ivory in poetry, but milk suggests a rather banal or at least domestic frame of reference. Ladies' hips are not usually mentioned in polite literature.

Her upper body is covered by a smock, embroidered front and back, as is her black silk collar on both sides. The collar is black as coal, another domestic image, but by now the reader is beginning also to notice that Alison is wearing rather a lot even according to the fashions of the time. Fourteenth-century women, and men, did wear more layers of clothes than modern people in order simply to keep warm, but Alison's clothes are elaborately decorated as well. Chaucer pushes the reader into noticing this by the fussy statement of 'bifoore/ and eek bihinde', split across two lines (lines 130–1), followed by 'withinne and eek withoute' in the line immediately following. He then adds that the tapes holding on her cap matched her collar, and that she wore a broad headband set high off her brow (lines 134–5). With that, the description reaches the top of her head. The final details of what she is wearing are kept until almost last: on her collar she wears a huge brooch, the size of the central boss on a shield, and her shoes are laced high up her legs (lines 157–9).

The overall effect of the description of Alison's clothing suggests that she is neatly and fashionably overdressed. As bits and pieces of haberdashery are added to the picture of this sexy young girl, the effect is of a reverse striptease. Its purpose may be, as the images suggest, to **satirise** the social class she comes from. She is wearing the cap and apron of a bourgeois housewife rather than a lady's veil, her clothes are overcontrived, her brooch is too big, and she is showing too much forehead and too much leg. Alison may be fair, but she is no lady, as the rest of the description bears out.

The modest stereotype of the courtly lady has grey eyes and blonde hair. Here Absolon has the ideal lady's colouring, though his greyness of eye is compared not to the dove but the goose (lines 206–9). Alison is dark, and although the **imagery** goes on suggesting that she comes straight from nature, she is more studiedly artificial than the ideal with plucked eyebrows (line 137) and a provocative look in her eye (line 136). Nonetheless, she presents an attractive physical picture if only because of her liveliness.

Images of fruit are used to suggest sexual ripeness – eyebrows black as sloes (line 138), her breath sweet as apples (line 156), her whole person looking like a pear tree (line 140). This is balanced by youthful freshness and friskiness suggested by comparisons with young animals: she is softer than young sheep's wool (line 141), playful as a kid or calf (lines 151–2), restless as a colt (line 155). Later when accosted by Nicholas she will initially shy away from him like a colt resisting breaking (line 174). Again these images are all drawn from a countryside domestic setting, wholesome but not exotic. Above all she is accessible. The sexiness of the picture that builds up is achieved by allowing the reader to get close enough to Alison imaginatively to feel how soft she is and to smell her breath and decide whether it is more like apples or honey. She is not demure: her voice is like the cry of the swallow nesting under the eaves of a barn in the same farmyard (lines 149–50), and the reader will later learn that when she does make her voice heard it is always at full emphatic pitch (lines 177–9 and 600–5). She is colourful, despite being dressed in black and white, as the narrator describes her **metaphorically** as a primrose and a pig's eye, both pretty wild flowers (one real, the other a joke flower) if not quite the roses used to describe the ladies of Romance or the lilies associated with the Virgin Mary.

Not all the description of Alison is of innocent natural sexiness, however. She is a married woman and, though her husband may be old, he is rich. The reader cannot miss, as the viewer would not, the leather purse that hangs at her waist, with its silk tassels and brass beading. To carry money so obviously is the mark of someone who is not accustomed to having it, and brass is a substitute for gold. The suggestion that Alison is petit bourgeois is built up by both metonymic (the purse) and metaphoric associations with money. Her face shines like a new 'noble' straight from the mint (lines 147–8), a coin worth just one third of a sovereign or pound, a modest but respectable sum of money.

In fact Alison has a precise economic value. She has married money, presumably elevating herself in the world, by taking on an elderly husband, a common enough practice at the time. There may be a suggestion that she is a country girl in origin only lately come to town, although all the rural references associated with her are metaphorical rather than actual. The last two lines retrospectively turn the whole description to an exercise in weighing and measuring as they sum up her exact social and economic value: being pretty, she might catch a lord as her lover. But looks cannot entirely overcome class or lack of it. The reader has already been softened into seeing her as a 'popelote', a pet, but the rhyme word in the same line reminds that she is also a wench (line 146), so fit to be a farmer's wife at best (line 162).

The whole portrait is a mixture of celebrations of Alison's whole-
someness and some rather snobbish jibes about her social status. Equally
she is a mixture of the innocent young and soft girl, and the knowing,
seductive wife, capable of calculating her exact worth.

TEXT *2*   (LINES 364–92)

> This Nicholas sat ay as stille as stoon,
> And evere caped upward into the eir.   365
> This carpenter wende he were in despeir,
> And hente him by the sholdres mightily,
> And shook him harde, and cride spitously,
> 'What! Nicholay! what, how! what, looke adoun!
> Awak, and thenk on Cristes passioun!   370
> I crouche thee from elves and fro wightes.'
> Therwith the night-spel seide he anon-rightes
> On foure halves of the hous aboute,
> And on the thresshfold of the dore withoute:
> 'Jhesu Crist and Seinte Benedight,   375
> Blesse this hous from every wikked wight,
> For nightes verye, the white *pater-noster!*
> Where wentestow, Seinte Petres soster?'
>   And atte laste this hende Nicholas
> Gan for to sik soore, and seide, 'Allas!   380
> Shal al the world be lost eftsoones now?'
>   This carpenter answerde, 'What seistow?
> What! think on God, as we doon, men that swink.'
>   This Nicholas answerde, 'Fecche me drinke,
> And after wol I speke in privetee   385
> Of certein thing that toucheth me and thee.
> I wol telle it noon oother man, certein.'
>   This carpenter goth doun, and comth agein,
> And broghte of mighty ale a large quart;
> And whan that ech of hem had dronke his part,   390
> This Nicholas his dore faste shette,
> And doun the carpenter by him he sette.

The opening of this passage is high drama. Amidst panic and commotion Robyn has just knocked down Nicholas's door so that he can be rescued. The door falls to the floor, but Nicholas, the consummate actor, does not flinch but sits as still as a stone (line 364). Although Nicholas appears passive, the reader is aware that this is the climax of his plot to deceive John and that all the activity has effectively been stage-managed by him.

In what follows, Chaucer alternates action with speech. The use of John's voice and imitation of his manner allow the reader to continue to build up a picture not just of him, but of the world he inhabits, and his whole, rather sparse, mental furniture. His confusion is in marked contrast to Nicholas's supreme control of the situation. The opening verse paragraph reveals the contrast between the two simply by the verbs it uses. It is a passage of pure action, but one in which Nicholas sits and stares, while John jumps to conclusions ('wende'), seizes him by the shoulders, shakes him and shouts at him (lines 364–9). Throughout what follows, John is constantly on the move while Nicholas stays in the same place. This characterises Nicholas's way of proceeding throughout the Tale: he repeatedly instigates actions which other people carry out for him.

The first words that John utters are probably intended to be seen as loud shouts in Nicholas's ear, trying to call him back from wherever his spirit has apparently gone. Superstitious John is frightened but resourceful within his limited understanding of the supernatural. He tells Nicholas to think of Christ's Passion and then makes the sign of the cross over him as a charm against the random assortment of evils that occur to him, not unlike making the sign of the cross to ward off vampires (line 370). Elves belong to children's stories and 'wights' is a vague word meaning little more than 'beings'. John has little notion of the theology and metaphysics of evil, but is vaguely aware that the unseen world has a nasty side, so is here being quite brave. He adds a charm against nightmares.

John's ensuing precautions against evil spirits prepare the reader for his willingness to accept that he has been chosen as the second Noah. He has a very approximate, ill-educated and childlike grasp of everything to do with religion, despite his work as carpenter at one of the country's great religious houses (see lines 556–60). During Chaucer's lifetime the question of how well the institution of the church was serving the ordinary people had become an issue. Radical elements wanted to dispense with church hierarchy, make sure all priests were educated, and translate the Bible and service books into English, but they were condemned as heretics as the church closed ranks to protect its interests. The radical movement, dubbed Lollardy by its detractors, began in Oxford with the ideas of a theologian called Wyclif who initially attracted attention at court.

Chaucer may not have been an active sympathiser with radical reform, but he demonstrates in a number of his works a willingness to criticise the way in which the church short-changed the common people. One of the popular ways in which ordinary people like John did find out about religious matters if they could not understand the Latin of the church services, was to watch and participate in the mystery plays in which Absolon was such an enthusiastic player (line 276). That John can still muddle up Noah with Noel (line 726) is a rather damning indictment of all attempts to inform the lay people about their faith.

Nicholas is treated to John's repertoire of inappropriate prayers. First he says a version of the children's bedtime prayer which calls upon the four evangelists, Matthew, Mark, Luke and John to bless the four corners of the house. John's version appears to call on Christ and Saint Benedict. Saint Benedict founded western monasticism and may have come into John's head because the Abbey of Oseney was a house of the Benedictine order. At any rate, he says this prayer five times, once for each wall and once on the threshold where the door was before Robin knocked it down. He then says the 'white *pater-noster*'. Again no critic is absolutely certain what this is, but the consensus is that it is another children's prayer, perhaps, 'Now I lay me down to sleep, / I pray the Lord my soul to keep'. '*Pater-noster*' is Latin for 'Our Father' and usually refers to The Lord's Prayer. John finally calls upon St Peter's sister, an obscure reference, as St Peter is not reported to have had a sister.

Pedantic attempts to discover the precise content of John's prayers, though no doubt interesting, are surely beside the point here. Chaucer is building up a comic dramatic situation, as well as the general conviction in the reader that John is an infant in matters of metaphysics and religion. The carpenter earnestly busies himself about the elaborate task of amateur exorcism, for which he is ill-equipped. Nicholas remains stock still.

Finally Nicholas begins to sigh. He is described as 'hende' here, the adjective so often associated with him that it almost becomes part of his name. Here it is particularly **ironic**, as he is in the middle of an elaborate and malicious deceit of John. He speaks. The question he asks, designed dramatically to seem like the middle of a conversation Nicholas has been having with some extraterrestrial in his dream, contains just enough information to frighten John while still holding him in suspense.

John, worried by what he thinks he has heard, urges Nicholas to focus on God, like a working man (line 383). This refers back to John's earlier diatribe on the dangers of intellectual pursuits (line 347). Not only is John ignorant, he is proud of the fact and moralises ignorance as an appropriate spiritual condition. This has some foundation in contemporary theology, which taught that too much knowledge led to spiritual pride. John is an illustration of the reverse danger that, where there is no true knowledge of the ways of God, superstition fills the gap. The Tale broadly **satirises** three types of masculinity: physical labour, represented by John, intellectualism, seen in Nicholas, and the **courtly love** and fine manners affected by Absolon. All turn out to be socially constructed roles which have their pitfalls.

Nicholas then tantalises further by offering to tell John a secret that no-one else will know. This is irresistible for the gullible carpenter who is quite happy to be imperiously ordered down several flights of stairs to get his lodger a drink. Their relative social positions are finely balanced here: John is the older, richer landlord, Nicholas the young, poor boarder, but superior knowledge confers a status which gives Nicholas the upper hand. The secret is to be conveyed 'in privetee', a word which appears often in the Tale. John (line 346), echoing the Miller (line 56), has only just asserted that men should not attempt to know God's 'privetee'. The reader knows that Nicholas is not interested in God's 'privetee'; it is Alison's 'privetee' which he wants to share with John.

John brings a quart of ale which they share companionably, preparing to talk man to man. Nicholas shuts the door – presumably picking it up from the floor first – and sits John down beside him. John is thus contained within Nicholas's private space and set up to be deceived by Nicholas's elaborate fantasy about the second Flood.

In comedy, pace and timing are very important. Nicholas here, by coming to slowly, starting his story in the middle, demanding a drink before he can go on, keeps not only John but the reader in an agony of suspense. John, whose voice the reader has already encountered making pompous statements about the dangers of dabbling with the supernatural (lines 340–59), is in this passage full of bluster and exclamation. The syntax of the passage is, therefore, very fragmented by the nature of the direct speech, and its division into short verse paragraphs also helps to create the impression of chaotic activity and panic.

TEXT 3   (LINES 615–51)

This Absolon doun sette him on his knees   615
And seide, 'I am a lord at alle degrees;
For after this I hope ther cometh moore.
Lemman, thy grace, and sweete brid, thyn oore!'
    The window she undoth, and that in haste.
'Have do,' quod she, 'com of, and speed the faste,   620
Lest that oure neighebores thee espie.'
    This Absolon gan wipe his mouth ful drie.
Derk was the night as pich, or as the cole,
And at the window out she putte hir hole,
And Absolon, him fil no bet ne wers,   625
But with his mouth he kiste hir naked ers
Ful savourly, er he were war of this.
Abak he stirte, and thoughte it was amis,
For wel he wiste a womman hath no berd.
He felte a thing al rough and long yherd,   630
And seide, 'Fy! alias! what have I do?'
    'Tehee!' quod she, and clapte the window to,
And Absolon gooth forth a sory pas.
    'A berd! a berd!' quod hende Nicholas,
'By Goddes corpus, this goth faire and weel.'   635

> This sely Absolon herde every deel,
> And on his lippe he gan for anger bite,
> And to himself he seide, 'I shal thee quite.'
> Who rubbeth now, who froteth now his lippes
> With dust, with sond, with straw, with clooth, with chippes,   640
> But Absolon, that seith ful ofte, 'Allas!
> My soule bitake I unto Sathanas,
> But me were levere than al this toun,' quod he,
> 'Of this despit awroken for to be.
> Allas,' quod he, 'allas, I ne hadde ybleynt!'   645
> His hoote love was coold and al yqueynt;
> For fro that time that he hadde kist hir ers,
> Of paramours he sette nat a kers;
> For he was heeled of his maladie.
> Ful ofte paramours he gan deffie,   650
> And weep as dooth a child that is ybete.

When the passage opens, John is temporarily forgotten, asleep in his kneading-trough in the roof, waiting for the Flood. Alison has taken control of the situation downstairs, finding herself with one lover in her bed but another one inconveniently making declarations of undying love to her outside the bedroom window. Absolon won't go away, so she bargains with him that she will give him one kiss, promising Nicholas that he will laugh his fill (lines 610–14).

The action moves outside and follows Absolon. We already know that the window is hinged and at chest height (lines 587–8). Absolon falls to his knees out in the street in the dark and continues to enact the courtly lover. In this position, his chin is roughly at window-sill height. He calls Alison his 'lemman', or sweetheart, not a particularly high-class word, and his sweet bird or bride, and asks for her grace and favour. The elaborate rhetorical construction of his speech, involving exaggeration, repetition with variation, and exclamation, makes him the more ludicrous because the reader knows what he looks like and how he is positioned. He feels like a lord and hopes that he will receive more than one kiss. He will receive more than he bargained for.

Alison's response is in sharp stylistic contrast to Absolon's way of speaking. Her main concern is that the neighbours do not see him (line 621). The desire to preserve her untarnished reputation unites her **ironically** (since she already has one lover in her bed) with the chaste heroines of courtly **Romance**, where secrecy is paramount.

Absolon carefully prepares to receive the kiss which is apparently the summit of his relatively innocent sexual ambitions. He has already chewed sweet-smelling herbs and put one under his tongue (lines 582–4), now he fastidiously wipes his lips dry (line 622). The narrator lingers thus on the detailed preparation for the kiss in the same way as Absolon himself will later savour the kiss itself.

The narrator's own voice intervenes to remind us that, although we have been picturing Absolon's position vividly, the night is so dark that in fact nothing can be seen at all. He uses two **similes**, dark as pitch and as coal, the same colour as Alison's black silk collar (line 132), although this is probably not significant since it is a common comparison. More significant is the rhyme of 'cole' with the entirely unexpected and shocking 'hole'. Chaucer more than once uses the rhymed couplet as a device to draw attention and to shock in this way: he will later rhyme 'kisse' with 'pisse' (lines 689–90).

Absolon seems to have little or no experience of amorous kissing and certainly does not sense very quickly that anything is amiss, but kisses Alison's naked backside 'ful savourly'. Again the choice of vocabulary connects with preceding information, as 'savour' contains within it connotations of tasting and smelling, of connoisseurship. Then the lingering kiss breaks off suddenly and Absolon jumps back. He may not know much about kissing, but he is a barber, so he knows that women do not have beards. He feels something with rough long hairs, and cries out in dismay. Devils are sometimes depicted in medieval illustrations with faces on their genitalia, and sexually alluring women are seen as devils set to lure men away from chastity and virtuous living. His cry takes the form of a question about what he has done, but his later action in borrowing the hot iron from Gervase the smith suggests that Absolon has worked out precisely what has happened to him. Alison's response is probably the most quoted line in the Tale (line 632). Many critics have chosen it as their favourite line in all Chaucer's work, with her cruel laughter and decisive slamming of the window. Alison's universally understandable 'Teehee!' is certainly, as one critic remarks, Chaucer's cruellest titter. It also continues to preserve something of the **paradoxical** innocence of

Alison and of Nicholas. They are less like corrupt adulterers, more like two children having fun playing a practical joke. If the Flood plot is Nicholas's doing, the misdirected kiss plot is of Alison's own devising and will turn out to be Nicholas's undoing when he tries to copy her quick wits.

The pun on 'berd' in the following line (634) is Chaucer's own to share with the reader, as Absolon did not speak aloud about Alison's 'beard'. Nicholas's exclamation (line 634) is a version of 'bourd', meaning trick or stratagem, or else the popular expression 'to make someone's beard', to make a fool of them. He is, as usual, referred to as 'hende', by now definitely meaning 'handy' and little else. Absolon, however, does hear Nicholas. He is described as 'sely' (line 636). The modern English 'silly' derives from this word, but, as with many little words in common use, the meaning has changed over time: Chaucer's 'sely' implies more 'innocent' than 'foolish'.

The moment is nonetheless Absolon's turning point, his dramatic conversion from effete courtly lover to avenger, as he walks off chewing his lips in wrath and swearing vengeance (lines 637–8). What Absolon lacks at this point is water to wash his mouth with. Nicholas too will soon have to cry out for water (line 707). Want of water holds the two plots in ironic tension and, for the observant reader, acts as a reminder of John in whose imaginative universe, were he awake, the whole world is currently under water. Absolon rubs his mouth with anything he can find lying around, straw, rags and wood-chippings, the sort of debris one would expect to find outside a carpenter's workshop, particularly one where John had recently hurriedly constructed three ladders (line 516). Absolon's flair for self-dramatisation now takes the form of a vow to dedicate his soul to the devil in order to secure revenge for his humiliation (lines 641–6). The succession of cries of 'Alas' shows him still speaking in artificial high style **rhetoric**, this time in **parody** of a formal lament, increasingly ludicrous given his circumstances. He fervently wishes he had turned away (line 645).

This section of the action finishes with the narrator's account of the change that comes over Absolon. His love is described **metaphorically** as formerly 'hot' but now 'cold' and 'quenched'. This unremarkable image is **proleptic** of what happens next, as Absolon borrows a hot iron which Nicholas requires water to quench. Chaucer rhymes 'ers' with 'kers' (lines 647–8), exploiting for his summary of what has happened the common expression *bais cul*, or 'kiss arse' common in carnival and farce (see Critical History, on Carnival). Love is described as a malady. In high Romance love indeed can be like a wasting sickness, though an ennobling one; for Absolon it has been an affliction which he is better off without. He wanders off cursing all lovers. But his experience has failed to make Absolon any older, wiser or more manly. He weeps like a child who has been beaten (line 651). The simile is reminiscent of his own earlier description of himself as a lamb crying after its mother's teat (line 596). His imagined 'Boo hoo!' for the reader chimes well with Alison's 'Teehee!' preventing, as Chaucer has warned, anyone from taking the whole story too seriously (line 78).

The passage expertly alternates action with the contrasting speech of Alison and Absolon, and narrative commentary. It also manipulates the use of the setting and visual perspective, as we see Absolon in the street, see the window through his eyes, see Alison and Nicholas rolling around in glee inside the house, and all the while preserve the knowledge that the scene is taking place in total darkness.

PART FIVE

BACKGROUND

GEOFFREY CHAUCER'S LIFE AND WORK

Geoffrey Chaucer was born in London in the early 1340s, most probably in 1343, the son, possibly the only son, of John Chaucer and his wife Agnes. The family originated in Ipswich where they had been called de Dynyngton or le Taverner and it seems likely that Geoffrey Chaucer's great-grandfather had been a tavern keeper. Geoffrey's grandfather, Robert de Dynyngton, appears to have worked for a merchant but when the merchant died in a brawl in 1302 Robert inherited some of his property. The family were now far more prosperous and as a result of this change in fortune they also changed their name. They took the name of their dead benefactor: Chaucer.

They settled in London where John Chaucer, Geoffrey's father, became a very prosperous wine merchant. He supplied wine to the king's cellars, supervising imports from France. He was influential and successful and was heavily involved in the business and political affairs of the city. His wealth and connections meant that he could provide his young son with many advantages, beginning with Geoffrey's enrolment as a page in the royal household.

A page was a boy between the ages of ten and seventeen who was an attendant in the house of a noble family. Effectively he was a servant but in this way a boy would learn about polite society and hopefully be accepted by a patron, someone who would take an interest in him and help his career. The young Geoffrey became a page to the Countess of Ulster, the king's daughter-in-law, and eventually served her husband, Prince Lionel.

It was in the service of Prince Lionel that Geoffrey was captured in France. Edward III made an unsuccessful attempt to gain the French throne in 1359 and Geoffrey Chaucer is named among those for whom a ransom was paid. After this, he seems to have entered the direct service of the king though his diplomatic skills seem to have been more in demand than his military expertise. He was sent on diplomatic missions to Spain, France and Italy over the next few years and some of his business appears to have been of a very secret nature.

Chaucer's social standing was also improved by his marriage in 1365 to Philippa Pan (or de Roet), a lady in the household of Queen Philippa, Edward III's wife. Philippa's sister Katherine was the mistress, and eventually the third wife, of John of Gaunt, the rich and powerful son of Edward III. Chaucer's marriage to Philippa therefore connected him more intimately to the rich and powerful circle of John of Gaunt and the royal court. John's son by his first marriage would later become King Henry IV and Chaucer's nephews were therefore half-brothers of the future king.

However, Chaucer's daily life does not seem to have been drastically affected by his family connections. In fact, in 1374 he was appointed to a new position with the customs department in London, a move which took him away from court. He was responsible for checking the quantities of wool, sheepskins and hides being shipped abroad so that the correct export duty could be charged. He was still sent overseas on state business and these trips probably brought him into contact with the works of the great European poets.

In 1389 he was appointed to a new position: clerk of the king's works. Still a civil servant, his new post meant that he was in charge of overseeing the building and repair of the king's properties. He supervised the workmen, paid the wages and saw that the plans were properly implemented. However, paying the wages proved to be more of a problem than it sounds. Chaucer was robbed, certainly once but possibly three times in the space of four days, as he attempted to deliver the money. It may have been a relief, therefore, when he was instructed to give up the post a few months later.

Chaucer now retired from the king's service but he continued to receive annual payments from the court, together with gifts such as a fur-trimmed, scarlet gown from the future Henry IV and an annual tun (252 gallons) of wine from Richard II. An occasional poem on the state of his purse ensured that his pension arrived on time but most of his creative energy was focused on one work, *The Canterbury Tales*. This was the last decade of Chaucer's life. He died on 25 October 1400, *The Canterbury Tales* still unfinished. He was buried in one of the more humble chapels in Westminster Abbey but his body was later moved to the east aisle of the south transept, where he became the first tenant of 'Poets' Corner'.

CHAUCER'S OXFORD

Chaucer's connections with Oxford, the setting of *The Miller's Tale*, were chiefly with the university. One of his associates was the philosopher Ralph Strode, who was a fellow of Merton College. Merton was the base of a school of astronomers in whose work Chaucer took a keen interest, giving rise to his prose *Treatise on the Astrolabe* – a device for measuring – written for his young son Lewis who lived, and probably went to school, in Oxford. One of the same circle of astronomers at Merton was Nicholas Lynn, whose fashionable theories on the measuring of shadows Chaucer makes enthusiastic use of elsewhere. It has been suggested that Nicholas in *The Miller's Tale* was named after him (Pearsall, 1992).

All Chaucer's adult life was spent as a cosmopolitan Londoner, so his writing about small-town life draws on Oxford and Cambridge, the two medieval university towns with which he was familiar, both of them barely larger than villages by modern standards. Chaucer's picture of Cambridge, or to be precise the village of Trumpington just outside Cambridge, the setting for *The Reeve's Tale*, is considerably less appealing than the Oxford of *The Miller's Tale* (Bennett, 1974). Chaucer's connection with a circle of Oxford scholars may account for this; equally Cambridge and its surrounding fens represented the East Anglia which his family abandoned in his youth as they climbed the social ladder.

CHAUCER'S OTHER WORKS

Chaucer's work spans most of the major genres of medieval literature. The earliest works to survive are short ballads of love, although he is chiefly remembered as a narrative poet. Medieval authors tended to draw creatively on existing material which they saw as authoritative, rather than inventing new stories, so much of what Chaucer wrote he would have described as 'translation' – literally 'carrying across'. Sometimes his translations are indeed loosely translated reproductions of great works of European literature in English. This is the case with his earliest long work, the *Romaunt of the Rose*, a rendering of a long allegorical French poem about love, and his later *Boece*, a prose translation of *The Consolation of Philosophy*, an influential Latin work by the early Christian philosopher Boethius.

Elsewhere, however, Chaucer drew on old stories from the European tradition, creatively adapting them in his own ways to make them fit different narrative contexts and voices, and to convey new meanings. He wrote three 'dream visions', narratives in which the narrator tells of a dream he had which has cast particular light on a subject. The first of these, *The Book of the Duchess*, offered John of Gaunt oblique consolation on the death of his first wife, Blanche. *The Parlement of Fowles*, in which the dreamer sees a variety of species of birds debating the nature of romantic love, was probably written for a Valentine's Day event at court. The unfinished *House of Fame* has the dreamer 'Geffrey' carried into the heavens by an eagle to find out what is the appropriate material for poetry. In *The Legend of Good Women* the poet dreams that the God of Love rebukes him for telling stories of unfaithful women, and this encounter is followed by a collection of narrative accounts of the lives of female saints and martyrs. As a series of tales set within a unifying framework it offers a model which he was to re-use more adventurously in *The Canterbury Tales*.

A number of other unfinished poems and fragments of Chaucer's writing have survived, as well as his scientific prose *Treatise on the Astrolabe*. Chaucer's longest single narrative poem, however, is the great tragic love story of *Troilus and Criseyde*, set in antiquity during the war between Troy and Greece, which tells the story of Troilus, younger son of King Priam of Troy, how he fell in love with the beautiful Criseyde, daughter of the disgraced Calchas who had betrayed the city. Troilus, with the help of Criseyde's uncle Pandarus woos and wins Criseyde, only to be deserted when she is sent over to the Greeks in exchange for a Trojan prisoner and seeks refuge in the arms of the Greek warrior Diomede. The poem incorporates philosophical commentary, high drama, and some of the most beautiful lyrical love poetry of its age.

The Canterbury Tales

Chaucer died before he could finish *The Canterbury Tales*, but he did write an ending for the whole book in which he dedicated his life and writings to God. Here he commended his philosophical and religious writing, but retracted what modern readers consider his best work, his narrative fictions, the dream visions, *Troilus and Criseyde*, and those of *The Canterbury Tales* that 'incline to sin'. *The Canterbury Tales* was his hugely ambitious last project.

The framing narrative has a number of pilgrims meet in the Tabard Inn in Southwark to undertake a pilgrimage to the shrine of St Thomas à Becket in Canterbury Cathedral. Pilgrimages to the shrines of saints were a popular contemporary way of repenting for sins committed and for making peace with God in what was a pervasively Christian age. Many involved great danger and hardship, and English men and women set off on journeys, from which they often did not return, to the shrine of St James at Compostella in northern Spain, to Jerusalem and to Rome. The journey to Canterbury was not, however, a hard one, especially in springtime, so the possibility for a **satirical** treatment of the pilgrims is present in Chaucer's account from the beginning. The motives of many for undertaking this supposedly penitential journey to England's most popular shrine are unclear; for many it seems to be a holiday outing.

The pilgrims represent a wide cross-section of Chaucer's contemporary society, but not one which is complete or ordered in any way, either socially or morally. Rather the reader finds a variety of medieval people defined by their way of life or occupation. The game they become involved in is a story-telling competition whereby each pilgrim is to tell two stories on the way to Canterbury, two on the way back.

The scheme was never completed and scholars continue to argue about the intended order of the Tales. None survives in Chaucer's own hand, and the manuscripts in which they were collected after his death arrange them differently. *The General Prologue* is there as a map, however, and the Parson's prose sermon appears before the author's epilogue. In the middle there are a number of fragments containing stories of knights and ladies in love, of tragedy, religion, and many riotously funny and sometimes obscene, narrative jokes. Some of the Tales stand alone, but many are grouped or paired. *The Knight's Tale*, a long aristocratic **Romance**, is first, linked to and followed by the sharply contrasting *Miller's Tale* and that of his rival the Reeve.

Many people in Chaucer's time saw signs of the expected end of the world. England was engaged in chronic warfare with France in what later became known as the Hundred Years War. Turbulence in Europe had led to schism in the Roman Catholic church, the one recognised church, so that from 1378 for a while there were two popes, one based in the Vatican, the other in Avignon in southern France. The middle of the fourteenth century had seen violent changes in the weather, with storms causing structural damage and years of ruined harvests. But, above all, the outbreak of the plague, later known as the Black Death, had wiped out around one third of the population of Europe during the 1340s. No wonder people believed that God might be angry.

The Black Death not only caused psychological shock to all in society, but hastened social change. The structure of government and the economy in England had been based since the Norman Conquest of 1066 upon landownership, with aristocrats and country gentry holding land from the King according to their place in the hierarchy. In return for landownership the King demanded military service as well as taxes to support the nation in peace and at war. The Church had a very similar structure. Archbishops and bishops were its great lords who acted as ministers, diplomats and advisers to the monarch. The church too supported itself by landownership by diocese, monastery or parish, each with its tenants. Those who prayed and those who fought made up the first two of the three 'estates', which was how contemporary theorists saw society. Those who worked, that is everyone else, made up the third estate.

The third estate had long ceased to be made up of peasants, however, but also included fabulously wealthy international merchants and well-to-do urban craftsmen. The growth of a varied urban life with its own complex social structures, and of a monetary economy where wealth could be measured not by land but by cash, was accelerated by the Black Death. The death of so many of the population assisted the collapse of old structures by creating a labour shortage and, consequently, greater social and geographical mobility. Many of Chaucer's pilgrims represent 'new money', only the Knight and the Squire representing the old ruling class. The Miller owes his position to old structures which depended on a captive immobile peasant population and a great manor house compelled to use their local mill. But he too knows the value of cash and has both the freedom and the means to come to London to go on pilgrimage.

Symptomatic of the pace of social change was the so-called Peasants' Revolt of 1381, actually a number of regional violent risings in Kent, East Anglia, and ultimately across the Home Counties and as far north as Yorkshire in the east. The crisis seems to have been triggered by the introduction of a new flat-rate poll tax as the Crown desperately tried to raise more money to sustain the war with France, but the demands of the rebels were various, and by no means all the rebels were peasants. At the climax a band of rebels marched into London, dragged the chancellor and treasurer of England out of the Tower where they were hiding, and beheaded them. They also burned down John of Gaunt's fabulous palace at the Savoy. The rebels entered London at Aldgate where Chaucer lived.

Richard II was king during the crisis of 1381. At the time he was only fourteen years old, having inherited the throne from his grandfather Edward III. Richard's father, also Edward, the Black Prince had tragically died the year before his father. The Black Prince had been the great warrior hero and model of chivalry credited with major victories against the French in the middle of the century. Richard inherited an unstable country, impoverished by war, which he never fully controlled. His uncle, John of Gaunt, Duke of Lancaster, remained the wealthiest and most powerful man in the kingdom. After a turbulent reign Richard was finally deposed in 1399 in favour of John of Gaunt's son, who became Henry IV. Richard died in mysterious circumstances at Pontefract Castle while in the custody of, among others, Thomas Chaucer, the poet's son.

URBAN LIFE

The Oxford setting of *The Miller's Tale* provides a very detailed picture of a substantial urban dwelling. Master craftsmen like John tended to live in the area of the town centre frequented by others engaging in the same trade and members of the same guild. Street names in some older cities are a reminder of this practice: Ironmonger Row, Tanners Hill, Baker Street. Each area formed a parish, and members of a craft would worship together in the same parish church which was the hub of their community. The successful craftsman typically employed one or two 'journeymen', qualified craftsmen who did not own their own workshop, and an apprentice. The craftsman's workshop was usually integral to his house, or tenement, which was likely to be a tall one, sometimes with jetties so that the upper floors could extend further over the street than the ground floor, to get more living room on to a small site. Houses and workshops were often very cramped together in order to accommodate as many as possible within the city boundaries or walls where protection and basic amenities were available. Neighbours would all know one another's business and there would be, as the Tale suggests, very little privacy.

It is possible, however, that Chaucer intends us to think of John as living in a larger house in the suburbs with a walled garden, maintained by taking in lodgers which were plentiful in a university town. A blacksmith's shop like Gervase's would be located away from the centre of population because of the risk of fire. The description of the house is tantalisingly both detailed and imprecise. The main communal area would have been the great hall, here, as we know from John's fall, extending from ground to roof beams. Built on behind it are the stables, and behind them an enclosed garden. John and Alison's bedroom is situated at the front on the ground floor, but in a part of the house divided into different levels. Nicholas's chamber is somewhere upstairs. The list of things on which Absolon wipes his mouth, including wood-shavings, provides the merest hint that John had a workshop on the premises, as would be expected, probably at lower ground-floor level on the street side.

LITERARY BACKGROUND

FABLIAU

The Miller's Tale is said to belong to the genre of medieval narrative known as **fabliau**. The fabliau was a form of verse narrative in vogue in France in the thirteenth century, written by and for the entertainment of aristocrats. It poked fun at the customs and social-climbing habits of the urban middle classes. The typical fabliau is racy in pace, often obscene in the focus of its action, and rarely if ever stops to indulge in description of character or setting. It usually centres on a practical joke, often a rude one, as the focus of the action. Its chief purpose is to make its audience laugh. If there was a pure English tradition of fabliau-telling in the same period it was oral, for little or nothing written survives.

A synopsis of the events of *The Miller's Tale* places it in the purest tradition of fabliau. It is a protracted joke with a punchline, as John falls from roof to floor cuckolded by the young wife he was vain enough to believe he could retain. The process of getting to this point has been by means of an elaborate practical joke perpetrated by Nicholas upon John which pokes fun at the intellectual inadequacies of the latter. The practical joke has involved liberal quantities of sexual and lavatorial humour.

However, in no fabliau does the narrator stop to describe his heroine in loving physical detail. This is the business of **Romance**. Even the portrait of Absolon, although it is the matter of pure burlesque, lies outside the range of fabliau telling, where the audience is left to form opinions of the characters by their actions and without the luxury of descriptive interventions by the narrator. The real difference is, however, the narrator himself, for the Miller, far from being the conventional superior young man set up to tell a risqué tale about his social inferiors, has stepped straight out of the fabliau himself. The Miller is the archetypal fabliau character. He is a know-all who believes that he can match the Knight's tale-telling expertise. He is all brawn and no brain, and even the things that he excels at – wrestling and bagpipe playing – effectively condemn him socially as someone who could never be received in polite society.

Chaucer's new departure is to put fabliau stories into the mouths of fabliau characters, then to lace them with low-life versions of the embellishments more common in Romance. What he creates is a more egalitarian type of comic tale-telling, but also an opportunity for dramatised narrative competition, or 'quiting', as the jokes no longer move in one direction only. Hence, if the Miller can tell a fabliau about a carpenter, the Reeve, a carpenter by trade, can retaliate with what is probably an even more obscene tale about an even stupider miller. Chaucer's original audience would have been courtiers, but there is evidence that as the fifteenth century progressed, his fabliau tales became popular with the upper bourgeoisie, the very class they **satirise**, confirming the opinion of critics who follow Bakhtin in the view that ultimately laughter has a universal character (see Critical History, on Carnival).

Sources

In constructing the plot of *The Miller's Tale*, Chaucer combines three story types. The first is the Flood, or the story of the man who was persuaded that he had been selected to be the second Noah. The second is the Misdirected Kiss, or the story of the lover who, expecting to kiss his loved one's mouth, was tricked into kissing a backside. And the third is the Branding, or the story of the adulterous lover who was branded on his bare backside by his rival. Two German, one Italian and one Flemish analogue have been found for these elements in the story.

The Italian story offers the most striking parallels. In it a carpenter has a young wife with three lovers, a Genoese, a priest and a blacksmith. When the blacksmith arrives at the house and calls out to the lady, claiming he is covered in sweat, the priest imitates her voice. The first lover is so scared by all the sound of love-making that he jumps out of a window and breaks his leg. The surviving version of this story dates from 1476, almost a century after *The Miller's Tale*.

The Flemish story is much nearer in date to Chaucer's writing, has fewer of the narrative details but is closer in the wording of some details, particularly the call for water as the smith-lover brands the priest-lover on his backside. Both German narratives contain other details but are much later still in date. It is assumed that all four are chance survivors and, like *The Miller's Tale*, versions of the same popular European bawdy story. All closely resemble *The Miller's Tale* in aspects of their plot, but none attempts its development of character nor links the different fabliau elements together verbally, so cleverly.

Romance

The Miller bullies the host into letting him tell his Tale when he does by claiming that it matches *The Knight's Tale* and picks up on the same subject. The designation of the Miller, his drunken state, and our glimpse at his initial attitude to sexual relations in his debate with the Reeve, indicate that within the drama of the tale-telling game at least, all his claims are highly improbable. But the ways in which *The Miller's Tale* expands on and embellishes the literary genre of the fabliau, if not its social world, owe everything to aristocratic Romance, of which *The Knight's Tale* is an elaborate example. As well as being a sophisticated and inventive contribution to the fabliau genre, *The Miller's Tale* in context is a parody Romance.

The introduction of the heroine in aristocratic Romance, the main object of desire and competition for the male protagonist (see Themes, on Love), involves the convention of *effictio*. The narrative stops and she is described in physical detail using highly conventional similes and metaphors. Typically she has hair like spun gold or the rays of the sun, skin like ivory, cheeks like roses and lips like coral. If she is animated at all, she has a soft low and tuneful voice, is moderate in all she says and does, and moves modestly. Chaucer draws on this convention when he describes Alison, and, although he reverses many of the characteristics of the ideal courtly lady and draws his images from the domestic rather than the exotic frame of reference, he stops short of parody because he imbues her with such frank vitality. Heroes too are sometimes subject to *effictio* in Romance, but always in terms of their character and conquests rather than the finicking details of their personal appearance: Chaucer's description of Absolon, because it follows the convention for the description of the female, is more truly parodic.

Romances tend to be rather long, not only because they indulge in long passages of static description and set-piece speeches, but because of their complicated plotting. Whereas the fabliau is a relatively simple narrative which progresses inexorably and single-mindedly to its punchline, the Romance keeps several plots going at the same time. This mastery of simultaneous action, which switches between location and situation, bringing them together finally for the narrative climax, was a speciality of French Romance writers and called *entrelacement* or interlacing. Chaucer, showing off his skills in narrative plotting, follows by turns what Alison and Nicholas are doing and what Absolon is up to at the same time. This relatively sophisticated handling of narrative structure also owes more to high Romance than it does to the more structurally straightforward fabliau.

ANTIFEMINISM

Antifeminism is endemic in medieval literature about relationships between the sexes. Fundamentally, woman in the eyes of the church carried the blame for the loss of Paradise because, according to the Book of Genesis, Eve had accepted the fruit from the serpent in the Garden of Eden. Eve provided the treacherous stereotype, only to be countered by the Virgin Mary who in being both virgin and mother, supplied an impossible role model. Chaucer's celebrated contribution to the debate is his Wife of Bath, a strong proponent of the cause of women but one whose characterisation depends heavily upon the very same unflattering images of women which she attacks men for creating.

In a society where many marriages were arranged, and death in childbirth was common, many men might marry a series of women throughout their lives, each of whom had to be of child-bearing years in order to ensure the survival of an heir. Consequently the unsuitable marriage of the rich but sexually feeble old man to the young, attractive sexy woman was common in antifeminist fiction and was known as the *senex amans*, literally 'old man lover'. It provides the whole plot for *The Merchant's Tale*, and is drawn on to provide the central causal pattern in *The Miller's Tale*. The Miller's philosophising introduction to his Tale (lines 43–58) indicates that the age difference between John and Alison is no accident of the plot, but is the recognisable antifeminist stereotype. As in all such tales of the *mal marié* – literally 'badly married' – the action presupposes that the old husband is impotent or sexually feeble. He is, therefore, jealous and keeps the young wife a virtual prisoner (lines 116–19). She is invariably sexually frustrated. The woman is portrayed either as an unprincipled sexual opportunist or as so stupid and gullible that she can be seduced by anyone who comes along. Her husband's anxieties are then justified, for, when he is unavoidably away from home, she flies straight to the arms of a young lover.

The antifeminism of these accounts draws on the story of the conception of Christ in Matthew's gospel where Joseph returns from a journey, finds the Virgin Mary pregnant, but is immediately reassured of her virtue by an angel. Retellings of the Nativity, particularly in late medieval religious plays, often reflect the influence in turn of the *mal marié*, by having an unenlightened Joseph lament his lot to an audience assumed to sympathise with his plight, the common lot of all old husbands. Because most young women fall short of the Virgin Mary, man should, as it is put in *The Miller's Tale* 'wedde his similitude' (line 120). John had not read Cato, a learned authority on the subject, and is, moreover, too vain and stupid to perceive that the message is one requiring no learned authority but simple common sense. What is best for woman is unconsidered as she is subject to the convenience of man.

PART SIX

CRITICAL HISTORY & FURTHER READING

Earlier criticism of *The Miller's Tale* was greatly preoccupied with its obscenity. The poet and playwright Dryden, writing in 1700, contributed more than most to the revival of interest in Chaucer, but chose to omit such 'immodest' material because he saw it as his duty to instruct rather than to please. Strutt, writing about the habits of the English in 1799, condemned *The Canterbury Tales* as a pilgrimage, outraged to find them 'deficient in morality and some few outrageous to common decency'. Even in the middle of the twentieth century, Robert Graves found in Chaucer's fabliaux evidence of his 'criminal sympathies' (Ross, 1983). Criticism thereafter has, fortunately, largely ceased to confuse the values of high art with those of public morality.

Chaucer criticism has diverged into a number of distinct approaches in the second half of the twentieth century. *The Miller's Tale* has attracted particular attention from critics who have been rereading Chaucer in relation to his historical circumstances (Marxist, New Historicist), from those working with theories of comedy (Carnival), and from a number of critics who focus on gender roles (Gender Studies). The work of many critics does not fit neatly into one category but fruitfully combines two or more approaches. The following range of approaches is not intended to be exhaustive but to represent some of the major currents of critical thought applied to *The Miller's Tale*.

HISTORICAL CRITICISM

Critics of this type, who are numerous, use the fourteenth-century context of Chaucer's work to illuminate aspects of its meaning. At its most extreme, historical criticism searches for real-life models for Chaucer's pilgrims (Manly, 1926). Most critics are less interested in that level of specificity but nonetheless focus on aspects of history to provide explanations for elements in the text. *The Miller's Tale* is systematically studied through its link within *The Canterbury Tales*, its relationship to the medieval genre of fabliau, the sources and analogues for its characters and plot, and its narrative structure. Its meaning is generated by placing it in a particular sequence, complementary to *The Knight's Tale*; in isolation it would be a tale without meaning (Cooper, 1989).

The contexts in which the genre of fabliau developed, and in which Chaucer adapted it for his own purposes, have preoccupied a number of critics (Brewer, 1975; Cooke 1978). The stratification represented particularly in *The General Prologue* has been explained in terms of contemporary satire on the medieval 'estates' system of understanding social organisation (Mann, 1973). Contemporary religious writing has been pressed into service to impose a pattern of moralised reading upon the sins and sinners in *The Miller's Tale* (Robertson, 1962); medieval astronomy has been investigated for illumination of the likely response of Chaucer's original audience to Nicholas's activities (Wood, 1970); and fourteenth-century Oxford has been explored to see what contribution setting makes to an understanding of the Tale (Bennett, 1974).

NEW HISTORICISM

Instead of viewing historical circumstances as an illuminating context for *The Miller's Tale*, New Historicism acknowledges the complex nature of history itself and the literary text itself as an historical event. Chaucer, seen by Humanist Criticism as broadminded and universal in his range of observation, is himself a phenomenon of the dynamic historical circumstances in which he lived (Patterson, 1997). *The Miller's Tale* is a witness to a number of competing elements which made up the culture of the late fourteenth century.

The Miller is chosen as the agent of disruption in *The Canterbury Tales* because millers had uncertain economic status, neither fully peasants tied by service to manorial estates, nor fully artisans free to trade where they pleased. It is not clear how prosperous they were, and, although it is known that they had a reputation for theft, it is again unclear whether their victims were mainly the lords or the peasants for whom they worked. There is evidence of millers participating in the Peasants' Revolt (see Historical Background), and the strength required for their occupation may contribute to their reputation for violence (Patterson, 1991).

The Miller's Tale is driven by political interests. It reflects circumstances more complex than a simple opposition between primitive agrarian society and new mercantile wealth and freedom. Economic vitality lay not with the oppressive merchant class but with middle-class peasants like the Miller himself. John, the prosperous rural carpenter, can be classified in this group. The representations of Nicholas and Absolon mock official culture: Absolon shows the church to be self-absorbed and comically ineffective, and Nicholas, seeking to demonstrate his superiority over working men, exposes those who claim to be Christians but live scandalous lives. John, like the rebels of the Peasants' Revolt, is robbed of an effective voice by being accused of madness, but the Tale's criticism of John also illustrates the stresses and strains within the working community. He allows himself to be intimidated by Nicholas and what he stands for, and he has married Alison. As a working man he should have a better command of common sense (Patterson, 1997).

The mixture of styles and genres in *The Canterbury Tales* is not just about artistic variety but also has a bearing on contending social assumptions specific to Chaucer's time. In opposition to *The Knight's Tale*, *The Miller's Tale* introduces a temporal, horizontal model of human society in which illusion is shown to be unnecessary baggage. It asserts the right of everyone to get on with their lives and to pursue self-advantage without interference. The Miller, a proponent of this kind of world, seems content with the justice of the conclusion, but Chaucer offers a last look at John which acts as a reminder of the damage that individualism can inflict. Although it illustrates a world which is the opposite of the Knight's, *The Miller's Tale* like *The Knight's Tale* offers both an embodiment and a critique of the social model it represents (Strohm, 1989).

MARXIST CRITICISM

Marxist criticism also focuses on the historical dynamics in which a work of literature was written, but it concentrates particularly on evidence of tension between social classes and the economic bases of power. Such critics see the relationship between *The Miller's Tale* and *The Knight's Tale* as more than **parody**; it is an exercise in **dialectic** between aristocratic and counter-aristocratic forces.

In *The Miller's Tale*, Nicholas, representing the professional classes, uses secrecy as a weapon to exploit the social group he is lodged with. Alison is a housewife, Absolon a man who does several jobs in the parish, Gervase works long hours, and John is a carpenter whose work takes him away from home. The hot coulter which brands Nicholas's backside is the weapon of revenge of the peasantry. The characters in *The Knight's Tale* try to contain disruption but do not value its agents; *The Miller's Tale* demonstrates the inner power of the world of churls. The Tale's real settings, concrete details, tightly controlled pattern of cause and effect and colloquial diction all demonstrate the confidence of the exploited class in their own materially real culture (Knight, 1986). Absolon' love-making deliberately clashes the idioms of aristocratic **courtly love** with his bodily frailties such as his need for a nap and his sweating. This need not be read only as making fun of Absolon; it also holds up to ridicule the pretentiousness of the aristocratic tradition which ignores normal bodily functions (Aers, 1986).

CARNIVAL

The translation into English of the writing of Russian cultural theorist Bakhtin (Bakhtin, 1968) greatly influenced the way which critics read comedy. Bakhtin used the example of medieval carnival festivities to demonstrate that laughter was a counter to, a safety valve against, the serious and official texts and ceremonies of church and state. Carnival – literally *carne vale*, 'meat farewell' – was originally the day of feasting and celebration which immediately preceded the long period of religious fast in Lent, and equates with modern Shrove Tuesday. Comic texts, like *The Miller's Tale*, are life-affirming and embrace everyone. The way in which they counterbalance official **discourses** extends beyond **parody** and is characterised by a project of systematic inversion. A common element in carnival humour is, therefore, the 'substitution of the face by the buttocks'. Carnival typically travesties official culture by transposing things normally associated with the upper body with the lower body in forms such as *bais cul* (kiss-arse). *The Miller's Tale* abounds in examples of carnival humour, in particular the use of courtly discourse to refer to sexual matters. There are also individual references, for example, to Alison's 'nether ye' (line 744).

A number of critics have read *The Miller's Tale* according to these principles. Music, dancing and springtime imagery create a sense of holiday which licenses what would otherwise be a coarse tale (Bennett, 1974). The range of the Tale's comedy is broader than parody, using sex as a reversal of the restraining forces of romance and religion, and blessing sexual indulgence as both simple and natural. It presents a world in which the search for knowledge ends in disaster brought about by vanity and folly, where there are no secret agents or astronomical influences to be found, where the world is simply a garden of delights to enjoy. The Tale thus has its own truth, 'the people's unofficial truth' (David, 1976).

HUMANIST CRITICISM

A number of critics focus on aspects of medieval literature which illuminate the human condition despite, rather than because of, historical circumstances. Chaucer uses the different genres available in the literature of his times to represent the manners and morals of a wide cross-section of society. The resultant achievement is artistic rather than moral (Jordan, 1967). In *The Miller's Tale*, he unfolds a comic fantasy full of rich characterisation, witty allusion, and versatile style, all pressed into the service of a marvellously engineered, ridiculous plot. The delight is not only in the final moment when the long-forgotten Flood-plot is reactivated by Nicholas's cry for water, but in the details involved in arriving at that moment, details which recreate imaginatively for us the house in Chaucer's Oxford (Pearsall, 1986).

More extreme, so-called New Criticism sees a knowledge of the Middle Ages as largely irrelevant or unnecessary to an understanding of texts, focusing on the language itself. The Miller is a device used to establish Chaucer's right to tell a comic tale. The Tale is pure farce in which the comic situation predominates. It exists for its plot rather than any moral or other meaning external to it (Craik, 1964). The variety of diction within the narrative, the contrast between language and situation are the mainspring of the humour (Donaldson, 1950).

DRAMATIC CRITICISM

Intermittently criticism of *The Canterbury Tales* focuses on a dramatic reading of the book. The major project of demonstrating how Tales relate to their tellers (Kittredge, 1915; Lumiansky, 1955) tends, however, both to ignore the complexity of the book as a whole, and to focus on the links between the Tales at the expense of the Tales themselves.

A theatrical reading of the Tales remains viable, particularly if its concern is the creation of dramatic voices within the Tales, rather than in the frame. *The Miller's Tale* has been read as a release of the popular voice and a dramatisation of its revolutionary force. Chaucer is here celebrating the potentially anarchic power of poetry and its performative properties, particularly when it makes proper language appear comic and promotes the brutal directness of popular wisdom (Gamin, 1996). The playing out of ambiguous gender roles, the focus on dressing up and playing a part, have also been highlighted as characteristics of the Tale which foreground its theatricality (Lomperis, 1995).

GENDER STUDIES

Feminist scholarship has been very active in offering readings of Chaucer's work. *The Miller's Tale* provides opportunities for feminist criticism as well as for a number of approaches which foreground issues of gender beyond the strictly feminist.

Fundamentally, the Tale demonstrates the economic basis of medieval marriage and the real limits of what someone in Alison's position can do with her sexuality. She is no victim, however, as sex is presented as fun throughout the Tale, a view which depends on the avoidance of deep emotional engagement (Martin, 1990). Alison's response to Nicholas's first approach is simply ritual female reluctance when faced by ritual male aggression. Absolon finds out that the language of love is not enough; that male desire must be assertive enough to carry responsibility for the sexual act. John's alleged imprisonment of Alison shows archetypal disregard for woman's freedom of being and action (Mann, 1991). Alison is a product and object of the male discourses that held power over women by controlling their bodies and language. When Alison sticks her backside out of the window she begins a chain of events which lead to the punishment of all three men who seek to control her. This is her gesture of defiance, using her body to speak out against the way in which she has been constructed by men (K.V. Donaldson, 1992).

But Alison may not be archetypally female at all: indeed no-one in the Tale inhabits his or her gender identity in a simple way. There is no evidence that Alison is caged by John, whose main attitude to her seems loving and protective. Ostensibly the Tale pits Nicholas's aggressive masculinity against Absolon's passive effeminacy, yet it is Absolon who wields the phallic coulter at the end. Alison is not so much a passive sex-object either, but seems to be Nicholas's willing partner. All the characters are highly theatrical, and cross-dressing characterised the medieval theatre. People gain attention in the Tale by their acting abilities, dressing up, role-playing and keeping up appearances. This may relate to fashions at the court of Richard II where heterosexuality may not have been the only acceptable sexual practice (Lomperis, 1995).

Certainly *The Miller's Tale* seems to see men who worship women according to the courtly love tradition as effeminate. All the men in the Tale seek to control their world through their own versions of masculinity: John is the working man who creates with his hands, Nicholas the intellectual who creates with his mind, Absolon is the courtly lover whose goal is to love women. All are vulnerable because their culturally constructed masculine roles depend upon assumptions about other men and about women, which turn out to be unreliable (Laskaya, 1995).

PSYCHOANALYTIC CRITICISM

The Miller's Tale has attracted the attention of psychoanalytical critics because Freud, the father of psychoanalysis, wrote extensively on the function of jokes. The Tale has been read as an improper 'joke-machine', built to let loose forbidden desires. It talks about sex and breaks down social boundaries, but at the same time channels all subversive urges into laughter. The joke itself can be seen as a sexual act, the punchline and ensuing laughter being the climax (Leicester, 1994). Jokes according to Freud generate psychical conformity. Viewed thus, the fabliau retrieves at a communal level the pleasure repressed by the kind of civilisation represented in *The Knight's Tale* (Knapp, 1990).

The Tale contains a number of Oedipal elements directed against paternal authority. Specifically Nicholas, a son-figure, turns the Bible, a patriarchal text, against John, the Tale's father-figure (Knapp, 1990). Alison is the focus for all responses in the Tale, as sex object, mother and child, but the reader is denied access to her 'privitee' as we never find out what she is thinking. She is an appendage to the men, but her rebellion is promoted by the masculine Miller (Leicester, 1994).

FURTHER READING

Information on many items in this list will be found in Critical History.

David Aers, *Chaucer, Langland and the Creative Imagination*, Routledge, 1980

– *Chaucer*, Harvester, 1986
> Marxist readings of social and economic circumstances satirised in Chaucer's work

Mikhail Bakhtin, *Rabelais and His World*, trans. Helen Iswolsky, Massachusetts Institute of Technology Press, 1968
> Early chapters apply carnival theory to medieval literature in general

J.A.W. Bennett, *Chaucer at Oxford and Cambridge*, University of Toronto Press, 1974
> Carnival or holiday spirit of *The Miller's Tale*; historical study of medieval Oxford as setting

D.S. Brewer, *Geoffrey Chaucer: Writers and their Background*, Ohio University Press, 1975
> Chaucer's writing in its historical context

Thomas D. Cooke, *The Old French and Chaucerian Fabliaux: A Study in their Comic Climax*, University of Missouri Press, 1978
> Historical study of Chaucer's source material

Helen Cooper, *The Canterbury Tales*, Oxford University Press, 1989
> Introduction to the tales, including sources and historical context

T.W. Craik, *The Comic Tales of Chaucer*, Methuen, 1964
Readings based on the principles of New Criticism: the Tales have no meaningful references beyond themselves

Alfred David, *The Strumpet Muse: Art and Morals in Chaucer's Poetry*, Indiana University Press, 1976
Carnival interpretation of the Tale, following Bakhtin

E.T. Donaldson, *Chaucer's Poetry: An Anthology for the Modern Reader*, 2nd ed. Ronald, NY, 1975
Readings according to the principles of New Criticism

Karla Virginia Donaldson, 'Alisoun's Language: Body, Text and Glossing in Chaucer's "The Miller's Tale"', *Philological Quarterly,*, 71 (1992) pp. 139–53
Feminist reading

John M. Gamin, *Chaucerian Theatricality*, Princeton University Press, 1996
Performance qualities of *The Miller's Tale*

Robert Jordan, *Chaucer and the Shape of Creation: The Aesthetic Possibilities of Inorganic Structure*, Harvard University Press, 1967
Humanist critical analysis of Chaucer's artistic achievement

George Lyman Kittredge, *Chaucer and his Poetry*, Harvard University Press, 1915
Dramatic Criticism relating tales directly to tellers

Peggy A. Knapp, *Chaucer and the Social Contest*, Routledge, 1990
Psychoanalytical analysis based on a carnival reading of *The Miller's Tale*

Stephen Knight, *Geoffrey Chaucer*, Basil Blackwell, 1986
Marxist interpretation

Anne Laskaya, *Chaucer's Approach to Gender in the Canterbury Tales*, D.S. Brewer, 1995

H. Marshall Leicester Jnr, 'Newer Currents in Psychoanalytic Criticism, and the Difference "It" Makes: Gender and Desire in the *Miller's Tale*', *English Literary History*, 61 (1994), pp. 473–99

Linda Lomperis, 'Bodies that Matter in the Court of Late Medieval England and in Chaucer's *Miller's Tale*', *Romanic Review*, 86 (1995), pp. 243–64
A reading of gender roles and sexuality in *The Miller's Tale* in historical contexts

R.M. Lumiansky, *Of Sondry Folk: The Dramatic Principle in the Canterbury Tales*, University of Texas Press, 1955
Dramatic Criticism relating tales directly to tellers

John M. Manly, *Some New Light on Chaucer*, Holt, NY, 1926
Investigating the possibility that there were real life models for the Canterbury pilgrims

Jill Mann, *Chaucer and Medieval Estates Satire: The Literature of Social Class and the General Prologue to the Canterbury Tales*, Cambridge University Press, 1973
Historical study arguing that the Canterbury pilgrims are satirical examples of the medieval 'estates'

– *Geoffrey Chaucer: Feminist Readings*, Harvester Wheatsheaf, 1991
Feminist reading of Chaucer

Priscilla Martin, *Chaucer's Women: Nuns, Wives and Amazons*, Macmillan, 1990

Lee Patterson, *Chaucer and the Subject of History*, Routledge, 1991

– '"No Man His Reson Herde": Peasant Consciousness, Chaucer's Miller, and the Structure of the Canterbury Tales', in Valerie Allen and Ares Axiotis, eds, *Chaucer: Contemporary Critical Essays*, New Casebook, Macmillan Press, 1997, pp. 169–92
New Historicist approach

Derek Pearsall, *The Life of Geoffrey Chaucer*, Blackwell, 1992
Critical biography of Chaucer

– 'The Canterbury Tales II: Comedy', in Piero Boitani and Jill Mann, eds, *The Cambridge Chaucer Companion*, Cambridge University Press, 1986
Humanist criticism

D.W. Robertson, Jr, *A Preface to Chaucer: Studies in Medieval Perspectives*, Princeton University Press, 1962

Thomas W. Ross, *A Variorum Edition of The Works of Geoffrey Chaucer*, Volume II, *The Canterbury Tales*, Part Three, *The Miller's Tale*, University of Oklahoma Press, 1983
    Major reference work with fully annotated text and critical history

Chauncy Wood, *Chaucer and the Country of the Stars*, Princeton University Press, 1970
    Specialist study of Chaucer's use of astronomy

World events	Chaucer's life	Literary events
1300 Population of British Isles: c. 5 million		
1309 Papal See moves to Avignon and comes under French control		
1313 Indulgences for public sale by Pope Clement V		

1315 Death of Jean de Meun, author of part 2 of *Roman de la Rose*, allegorical poem mocking love, women, the Church and those in authority

1319 Death of Jean de Joinville, French chronicler

1321 Edward II forced to abdicate, imprisoned and probably murdered. Edward III accedes to throne, with wife Philippa

1321 Death of Dante Alighieri, author of *Divine Comedy*

1330 Birth of John Gower, friend of Chaucer and author

1331 Birth of William Langland, author

1337 Birth of Jean Froissart, who will become Clerk of the Chamber to Queen Philippa, and author of *Chronicles*, a brilliant history of 14th-century Europe

1338 Beginning of 100 Years War between France and England

1341 Petrarch crowned as laureate poet at Capitol, Rome

1343? Birth of Geoffrey Chaucer in London

1346 French routed at Crécy by Edward III and his son the Black Prince

CHRONOLOGY

World events	Chaucer's life	Literary events

1349 Black Death reaches England and kills one third of population

1351 First Statute of Labourers regulates wages in England

1353 In Italy, Giovanni Boccaccio finishes his *Decameron*, a collection of 100 bawdy tales

1357 Chaucer in service of Countess of Ulster, wife of Prince Lionel, 3rd son of Edward III

1359 Edward III makes unsuccessful bid for French throne

1359 Serves in army in France, under Prince Lionel; taken prisoner

1360 Edward III pays ransom of £16 for Chaucer's freedom

1361 Black Death reappears in England

1362 English becomes official language in Parliament and Law Courts

1363 Birth of Christine de Pisan, French author of *La Cité des Dames*, listing all the heroic acts and virtues of women

1365 Marries Philippa Pan (or Payne) de Roet

1366 In Spain on diplomatic mission

1367 Granted life pension for his services to king; birth of his son Thomas

1368 On Prince Lionel's death, his services transferred to John of Gaunt, Duke of Lancaster

World events	Chaucer's life	Literary events

1369 In France with John of Gaunt's expeditionary force; begins *Book of the Duchess* on death of Blanche, John of Gaunt's wife

1370-3 Sent on diplomatic missions (11 months in Italy)

1370 *(c.)* William Langland's *Piers Plowman*

1374 Appointed Controller of the Customs and Subsidy of Wools, Skins and Leather; receives life pension from John of Gaunt

1375 *(c.)* *Sir Gawain and the Green Knight* written

1376 Receives payment for some secret, unspecified service

1377 Edward III dies and is succeeded by Richard II, son of the Black Prince

1377 Employed on secret missions to Flanders, and sent to France to negotiate for peace with Charles V; employed on further missions in France, Lombardy and Italy

1378 Beginning of the Great Schism: Urban VI elected Pope in Rome, Clement VII in Avignon

1380 John Wyclif, who attacked orthodox Church doctrines, condemned as heretic. Wyclif's followers translate Bible into vernacular

1380 *Parliament of Fowls* written; birth of son Lewis. Cecilia Chaumpayne releases Chaucer from charge of '*de raptu meo*'

1381 Peasant's Revolt under Wat Tyler quelled by Richard II

World events	Chaucer's life	Literary events
	1382 Appointed, in addition, Controller of the Petty Customs	
	1385 Allowed privilege of appointing deputy to perform his duties as Controller. Probably writes *Legend of Good Women* and *Troilus and Criseyde*	
	1385-99 Now living in Greenwich	
1386 Richard II deprived of power	**1386** Deprived of both official posts. Elected Knight of Shire of Kent	
	1387 Wife Philippa dies. Begins writing *The Canterbury Tales*	
	1388 In poverty, Chaucer sells his pensions to raise money	
1389 Richard II resumes power	**1389** Appointed clerk of king's works at Westminster	**1389** John Gower completes first version of *Confessio Amantis*
	1391 Writes *Treatise on the Astrolabe* for his son Lewis. Resigns as clerk of king's works and becomes deputy forester of royal forest at North Petherton, Somerset	
1396 John of Gaunt marries his mistress, Katherine (de Roet), Chaucer's sister-in-law		
1399 Richard II forced to abdicate. Henry IV becomes King of England		
1400 Richard II dies in prison. Population of British Isles *c.* 3.5 million	**1400** Chaucer dies	
		1450 Gutenberg produces first printed book in moveable type

allegory a story or situation with two or more coherent meanings

alliteration a sequence of repeated consonantal sounds

analogue a parallel word or thing; a story with a similar or comparable plot

apocrypha works of unknown authorship considered not authentic

apostrophe speech addressed to a person, idea or thing, often exclamatory

bombast turgid and inflated language (named after a type of cotton padding)

cliché boring phrase made tedious by constant repetition

couplet a pair of rhymed lines

courtly love love conducted according to system of high chivalric ideals courtly love one who follows this system

dialectic logical disputation; a progress of question and answer moving towards the truth

discourse a piece of writing; a framework of references relating to a specific topic or context

effictio description of physical detail of heroine and hero in a courtly Romance

entrelacement interlacing of several plots in a courtly Romance

euphemism polite word or phrase concealing blunt or crude meaning

fabliau comic tale in verse, characterised by bawdiness (see Literary Background)

farce dramatic writing intended to provoke laughter, entertainment its only motive

figure metaphor which stands for and reveals divine truths

genre a kind or type of literature; prose, poetry, drama and their subdivisions

iambic pentameter a line of five feet, each made up of one unstressed and one stressed syllable

imagery, images figurative language referring to objects and qualities which evoke a particular emotion or feeling

irony saying one thing but meaning something else

lament formalised expression of deep sorrow at death or loss

metaphor a comparison in which one thing is described as being another

Oedipal psychological theory that men retain infantile repressed desires for their mothers

paradox an apparently self-contradictory statement

parataxis the placing of clauses or sentences side by side without connections

parody imitation with the intent of ridicule

prolepsis anticipation of future events in narrative

register kind of language being used, particularly in relation to a situation

rhetoric the art of persuasive speech or writing

rime riche the rhymed syllable is repeated in its entirety, including the initial consonant

Romance medieval prose or verse dealing with adventures of chivalry and courtly love

satire writing that exposes wickedness or folly by holding them up to ridicule

simile a comparison in which one thing is described as being like another

subtext implicit assumptions or situation behind the explicit plot

syntax the arrangement of words in appropriate grammatical form and order

AUTHOR OF THIS NOTE

Pamela M. King is Professor of English and Head of Department at St Martin's College, Lancaster. She is a graduate of the Universities of Edinburgh and York, and taught for several years at London University. She has published widely on aspects of medieval literature and culture, and has a particular interest in the medieval theatre.

York Notes Advanced (£3.99 each)

Margaret Atwood
Cat's Eye

Margaret Atwood
The Handmaid's Tale

Jane Austen
Mansfield Park

Jane Austen
Persuasion

Jane Austen
Pride and Prejudice

Alan Bennett
Talking Heads

William Blake
Songs of Innocence and of Experience

Charlotte Brontë
Jane Eyre

Emily Brontë
Wuthering Heights

Angela Carter ‘
Nights at the Circus

Geoffrey Chaucer
The Franklin's Tale

Geoffrey Chaucer
The Miller's Prologue and Tales

Geoffrey Chaucer
Prologue To the Canterbury Tales

Geoffrey Chaucer
The Wife of Bath's Prologue and Tale

Joseph Conrad
Heart of Darkness

Charles Dickens
Great Expectations

Charles Dickens
Hard Times

Emily Dickinson
Selected Poems

John Donne
Selected Poems

Carol Ann Duffy
Selected Poems

George Eliot
Middlemarch

George Eliot
The Mill on the Floss

T.S. Eliot
Selected Poems

F. Scott Fitzgerald
The Great Gatsby

E.M. Forster
A Passage to India

Brian Friel
Translations

Thomas Hardy
The Mayor of Casterbridge

Thomas Hardy
The Return of the Native

Thomas Hardy
Selected Poems

Thomas Hardy
Tess of the d'Urbervilles

Seamus Heaney
Selected Poems from Opened Ground

Nathaniel Hawthorne
The Scarlet Letter

Kazou Ishiguru
The Remains of the Day

James Joyce
Dubliners

John Keats
Selected Poems

Christopher Marlowe
Doctor Faustus

Arthur Miller
Death of a Salesman

John Milton
Paradise Lost Books I & II

Toni Morrison
Beloved

William Shakespeare
Antony and Cleopatra

William Shakespeare
As You Like It

William Shakespeare
Hamlet

William Shakespeare
King Lear

William Shakespeare
Measure for Measure

William Shakespeare
The Merchant of Venice

William Shakespeare
A Midsummer Night's Dream

William Shakespeare
Much Ado About Nothing

William Shakespeare
Othello

William Shakespeare
Richard II

William Shakespeare
Romeo and Juliet

William Shakespeare
The Taming of the Shrew

William Shakespeare
The Tempest

William Shakespeare
The Winter's Tale

George Bernard Shaw
Saint Joan

Mary Shelley
Frankenstein

Alice Walker
The Color Purple

Oscar Wilde
The Importance of Being Earnest

Tennessee Williams
A Streetcar Named Desire

John Webster
The Duchess of Malfi

Virginia Woolf
To the Lighthouse

W.B. Yeats
Selected Poems

GCSE and equivalent levels (£3.50 each)

Maya Angelou
I Know Why the Caged Bird Sings

Jane Austen
Pride and Prejudice

Alan Ayckbourn
Absent Friends

Elizabeth Barrett Browning
Selected Poems

Robert Bolt
A Man for All Seasons

Harold Brighouse
Hobson's Choice

Charlotte Brontë
Jane Eyre

Emily Brontë
Wuthering Heights

Shelagh Delaney
A Taste of Honey

Charles Dickens
David Copperfield

Charles Dickens
Great Expectations

Charles Dickens
Hard Times

Charles Dickens
Oliver Twist

Roddy Doyle
Paddy Clarke Ha Ha Ha

George Eliot
Silas Marner

George Eliot
The Mill on the Floss

William Golding
Lord of the Flies

Oliver Goldsmith
She Stoops To Conquer

Willis Hall
The Long and the Short and the Tall

Thomas Hardy
Far from the Madding Crowd

Thomas Hardy
The Mayor of Casterbridge

Thomas Hardy
Tess of the d'Urbervilles

Thomas Hardy
The Withered Arm and other Wessex Tales

L.P. Hartley
The Go-Between

Seamus Heaney
Selected Poems

Susan Hill
I'm the King of the Castle

Barry Hines
A Kestrel for a Knave

Louise Lawrence
Children of the Dust

Harper Lee
To Kill a Mockingbird

Laurie Lee
Cider with Rosie

Arthur Miller
The Crucible

Arthur Miller
A View from the Bridge

Robert O'Brien
Z for Zachariah

Frank O'Connor
My Oedipus Complex and other stories

George Orwell
Animal Farm

J.B. Priestley
An Inspector Calls

Willy Russell
Educating Rita

Willy Russell
Our Day Out

J.D. Salinger
The Catcher in the Rye

William Shakespeare
Henry IV Part 1

William Shakespeare
Henry V

William Shakespeare
Julius Caesar

William Shakespeare
Macbeth

William Shakespeare
The Merchant of Venice

William Shakespeare
A Midsummer Night's Dream

William Shakespeare
Much Ado About Nothing

William Shakespeare
Romeo and Juliet

William Shakespeare
The Tempest

William Shakespeare
Twelfth Night

George Bernard Shaw
Pygmalion

Mary Shelley
Frankenstein

R.C. Sherriff
Journey's End

Rukshana Smith
Salt on the snow

John Steinbeck
Of Mice and Men

Robert Louis Stevenson
Dr Jekyll and Mr Hyde

Jonathan Swift
Gulliver's Travels

Robert Swindells
Daz 4 Zoe

Mildred D. Taylor
Roll of Thunder, Hear My Cry

Mark Twain
Huckleberry Finn

James Watson
Talking in Whispers

William Wordsworth
Selected Poems

A Choice of Poets

Mystery Stories of the Nineteenth Century including The Signalman

Nineteenth Century Short Stories

Poetry of the First World War

Six Women Poets

Chinua Achebe
Things Fall Apart

Edward Albee
Who's Afraid of Virginia Woolf?

Jane Austen
Emma

Jane Austen
Northanger Abbey

Jane Austen
Sense and Sensibility

Samuel Beckett
Waiting for Godot and *Endgame*

Louis de Bernières
Captain Corelli's Mandolin

Charlotte Brontë
Villette

Robert Browning
Selected Poems

Robert Burns
Selected Poems

Geoffrey Chaucer
The Merchant's Tale

Geoffrey Chaucer
The Nun's Priest's Tale

Caryl Churchill
Top Girls and *Cloud Nine*

Samuel Taylor Coleridge
Selected Poems

Daniel Defoe
Moll Flanders

Daniel Defoe
Robinson Crusoe

Charles Dickens
Bleak House

T.S. Eliot
The Waste Land

Henry Fielding
Joseph Andrews

E.M. Forster
Howards End

John Fowles
The French Lieutenant's Woman

Anne Frank
The Diary of Anne Frank

Robert Frost
Selected Poems

Elizabeth Gaskell
North and South

Stella Gibbons
Cold Comfort Farm

Graham Greene
Brighton Rock

Thomas Hardy
Jude the Obscure

Joseph Heller
Catch-22

Homer
The Iliad

Homer
The Odyssey

Gerard Manley Hopkins
Selected Poems

Henrik Ibsen
The Doll's House and *Ghosts*

Ben Jonson
The Alchemist

Ben Jonson
Volpone

James Joyce
A Portrait of the Artist as a Young Man

Philip Larkin
Selected Poems

Aldous Huxley
Brave New World

D.H. Lawrence
The Rainbow

D.H. Lawrence
Selected Poems

D.H. Lawrence
Selected Stories

D.H. Lawrence
Sons and Lovers

D.H. Lawrence
Women in Love

Christopher Marlowe
Edward II

John Milton
Paradise Lost Bks IV & IX

Thomas More
Utopia

Sean O'Casey
Juno and the Paycock

George Orwell
Nineteen Eighty-four

John Osborne
Look Back in Anger

Wilfred Owen
Selected Poems

Sylvia Plath
Selected Poems

Alexander Pope
Rape of the Lock and other poems

Ruth Prawer Jhabvala
Heat and Dust

J.B. Priestley
When We Are Married

Jean Rhys
Wide Sargasso Sea

William Shakespeare
As You Like It

William Shakespeare
Coriolanus

William Shakespeare
Henry IV Pt I

Wliiam Shakespeare
Henry IV Part II

William Shakespeare
Henry V

William Shakespeare
Julius Caesar

William Shakespeare
Macbeth

William Shakespeare
Measure for Measure

William Shakespeare
Richard III

William Shakespeare
Sonnets

William Shakespeare
Twelfth Night

William Shakespeare
The Winter's Tale

George Bernard Shaw
Arms and the Man

Muriel Spark
The Prime of Miss Jean Brodie

John Steinbeck
The Grapes of Wrath

John Steinbeck
The Pearl

Future titles (continued)

Tom Stoppard
Arcadia and *Rosencrantz and Guildenstern are Dead*

Jonathan Swift
Gulliver's Travels and The Modest Proposal

Alfred, Lord Tennyson
Selected Poems

W.M. Thackeray
Vanity Fair

Virgil
The Aeneid

Edith Wharton
Ethan Frome

Jeanette Winterson
Oranges are Not the Only Fruit and *Written on the Body*

Tennessee Williams
Cat on a Hot Tin Roof

Tennessee Williams
The Glass Menagerie

Virginia Woolf
Mrs Dalloway

William Wordsworth
Selected Poems

The Diary of Anne Frank

Metaphysical Poets